MORE THAN
MANAGING

MORE THAN MANAGING

THE RELENTLESS PURSUIT OF **EFFECTIVE JEWISH LEADERSHIP**

Edited by **Rabbi Lawrence A. Hoffman, PhD**

For People of All Faiths, All Backgrounds
JEWISH LIGHTS PUBLISHING
Nashville, Tennessee

Jewish Lights Publishing
an imprint of Turner Publishing Company
Nashville, Tennessee
New York, New York

www.jewishlights.com
www.turnerpublishing.com

More Than Managing:
The Relentless Pursuit of Effective Jewish Leadership

© 2016 by Lawrence A. Hoffman

Library of Congress Cataloging-in-Publication Data
Names: Hoffman, Lawrence A., 1942– editor.
Title: More than managing : the relentless pursuit of effective Jewish leadership / edited by Rabbi Lawrence A. Hoffman, PhD.
Description: Nashville, TN : Jewish Lights Publishing, [2016] | Includes bibliographical references.
Identifiers: LCCN 2016027472| ISBN 9781580238700 (hardcover) | ISBN 9781580238830 (ebook)
Subjects: LCSH: Jewish leadership. | Jewish leadership—United States. | Synagogues—United States—Organization and administration. | Leadership—Religious aspects—Judaism.
Classification: LCC DS140 .M67 2016 | DDC 303.3/4089924073—dc23 LC record available at https://lccn.loc.gov/2016027472

10 9 8 7 6 5 4 3 2 1

Manufactured in the United States of America

Cover Design: Adam Reiss
Interior Design: Thor Goodrich

To Leslie Wexner, a leader's leader.

CONTENTS

Acknowledgments   xi

Introduction

Leadership and the Jewish Condition   xiii
     Rabbi Lawrence A. Hoffman, PhD

Foreword

A Values Map: The Journey to Our Best Selves   xix
     Rabbi B. Elka Abrahamson

Part One
What Leaders Need to Know

Lessons on Leadership   3

Nudging as a Tool of Leaders   5
     Dr. Max H. Bazerman

The Power of Inclusion   9
     Patricia Bellinger

Purpose, People, and Principle: Leadership for the
   Unnatural Leader   13
     Dr. David T. Ellwood

Leading So You Get It Wrong   18
     Arna Poupko Fisher

The Epitome of an Authentic Leader   22
     Bill George

Jewish Adaptability, Authority, and Leadership   26
     Ronald Heifetz

The Heart of Darkness   31
     Dr. Barbara Kellerman

I've Never Experienced Anything Like the Times
   We Are In   35
     Marty Linsky

The Leader as Negotiator   40
     Dr. Brian Mandell

Leaders and Managers: Divergence and
   Convergence   44
     Larry Moses

Four Kiwis and the Jewish Future   48
  Rabbi Aaron Panken, PhD
Showing Up: The Power of Presence   52
  Rae Ringel
Riding the Mood Elevator   55
  Dr. Larry Senn
To Do or to Be: Leadership Lessons from the Court
  of St. James's   60
  Ambassador Daniel Taub

Jewish Models of Leadership   65
Leading Change: A Lesson from Tamar and Judah   67
  Maya Bernstein
What Do You Stand For?   71
  Dr. Erica Brown
Tears of Doubt: Rabbi Yochanan ben Zakkai's
  Spiritual Legacy   74
  Dr. Ruth Calderon
The Impossible Task of Jewish Leadership   78
  Rabbi Edward Feinstein
First Plant the Sapling: Beyond Messianic
  Leadership   82
  Rabbi Lisa J. Grushcow, DPhil
Solidarity Ethnic and Human: Moses and Moral
  Responsibility   86
  Rabbi Shai Held, PhD
The Moral Mandate of Community   90
  Dr. Yehuda Kurtzer
The Global Wrap of *T'fillin*: Touching Our Heart
  but Reaching the World   94
  Rabbi Asher Lopatin
Look Out Above! Keeping Values in Sight on Our
  Halachic Hike   97
  Rabbi Daniel S. Nevins
The God Who Loves Pluralism   101
  Rabbi Rachel Sabath Beit-Halachmi, PhD
Leading from Tents, Not from Arks   105
  Rabbi Joanna Samuels
Marshmallows, Ketchup, and Redemption: How
  Leaders Manage Expectations   108
  Rabbi Jacob J. Schacter, PhD
The Voice at the Table   112
  Susan K. Stern

Judge Away   115
  Rabbi Shira Stutman

Leadership and Confrontation: Lessons from Moses
  and God   119
  Rabbi Melissa Weintraub

Keep It Simple: The Three Stages of Change   123
  Rabbi Avi Weiss

"Let What Is Broken So Remain": Leadership's
  Lotus Hour   127
  Rabbi Mishael Zion

Part Two
The Jewish Condition

The Global View   133

Why Programs in Leadership? Why Now? A
  Historical Perspective   135
  Dr. Robert Chazan

Three Eras of Jewish History and Their Leaders   138
  Rabbi Irving (Yitz) Greenberg

The Jewish People's Story, Not Just My Own   143
  Dr. Deborah E. Lipstadt

Leadership for the New Era: The Challenge /
  The Opportunity   147
  Dr. John Ruskay

Challenges in Israel   151

Leader as Gatekeeper: Battling Corruption in a
  Diverse Democracy   153
  Avia Alef, Adv, LLM, MC-MPA

Speaking Up for Israel's Voiceless   157
  Sharon Abraham-Weiss, Adv, LLM, MC-MPA

Stop Feeling Sorry for Disabled Children
  (Start Respecting Them Instead)   160
  Dr. Maurit Beeri

Out of the Shtetl: A Mature, Confident, and
  Constructive Zionism   164
  Nadav Tamir

Gender in the IDF: Promoting Women Leadership
  in a Male Organization   168
  Brigadier General Rachel Tevet Wiesel

The Enduring Leadership of David Ben-Gurion,
Israel's Eternal "Old Man"   172
Major General (retired) Amos Yadlin

Challenges in America   177

American Jews Speak a "Jewish Language"   179
Dr. Sarah Bunin Benor

The Tones of Leadership   183
Dr. David Bryfman

Orthodox Jewish Feminism on the Rise: Offense Is
Your Best Defense   187
Dr. Sharon Weiss-Greenberg

The Quietly Insistent Entrepreneur   191
Peter A. Joseph

Model-Driven or Market-Driven? A Lesson from
Birthright Israel   195
Dr. Shaul Kelner

Student Lives on the Line: Moral Leadership in
Jewish Day Schools   199
Rabbi Judd Kruger Levingston, PhD

Part Three
Appreciation

Les Wexner, Harry Truman, and the Leadership of
Readership   205
David Gergen

Les Wexner and the Polar Bears   212
Charles R. Bronfman

Leadership: The Most Important Topic   216
Leslie Wexner

Conclusion

Ten Commandments for Leaders   221
Rabbi Lawrence A. Hoffman, PhD

Notes   224

ACKNOWLEDGMENTS

A great number of people went out of their way to create this book, in service to a vision and in recognition of the visionary. Acknowledgements begin, therefore, with gratitude to the visionary, Leslie H. Wexner. This gratitude to Les extends easily and naturally to Abigail, his wife and co-chair of the Wexner Foundation—the Foundation's thirtieth anniversary prompted the book in the first place. I am personally grateful to Les and to Abigail who extended themselves so graciously in making this book possible.

Les regularly draws lessons from biographies of great leaders. With that in mind, I cite a story told of Dwight D. Eisenhower's tenure as president of Columbia University. Upon ascending to the position, he assembled the faculty to get to know the people who worked there. The faculty chair is said to have contended, "Mr. President, we do not work at the university; we *are* the university." In similar fashion, the contributors to a book such as this actually *are* the book. If the book is graced with wisdom, it is because of the combined insights of its many authors—all of whom deserve profound recognition.

Books are not just written, however; they are produced, and in this case, production entailed the staffs of not just one but three collaborating institutions. First and foremost was the Wexner Foundation itself. As a long-time teacher for the Foundation, I am ever mindful of all the wonderful people who work there as a team and who support all of the foundation's work, this book included. I would love to include all their names, even though I single out here just the Foundation President, Rabbi B. Elka Abrahamson, and its Program Director, Rabbi Benjamin Berger. The two of them were my constant companions in planning and carrying out every facet of this book's planning, from determining its contents to making editorial decisions along the way. An editor could not hope for better partners.

On the production side, I am grateful to the staff at Jewish Lights Publishing in Woodstock Vermont, and subsequently, at Turner Publishing, to whom Jewish Lights was sold as the book entered production. With his customary farsightedness, Stuart Matlins, in Woodstock (the Founder and President of Jewish Lights), welcomed the project and involved himself directly in bringing it to fruition. Many members of his staff were involved thereafter, first and foremost, Emily Wichland, a managing editor who is every writer's dream. Deborah Corman gave generously of herself as copy editor. Tim Holtz at Jewish Lights and Adam Reiss at the Wexner Foundation worked together to produce the cover. At Turner Publishing, I happily express my gratitude to Todd Bottorff, President and Publisher, who welcomed this volume; to Marketing Coordinator Jolene Barto; to Executive Editor Stephanie Beard; to proofreader Lisa Grimenstein; and to Managing Editor Jon O'Neal, who graciously and competently brought this book into the world.

To one and all—I owe my deepest gratitude.

INTRODUCTION

Leadership and the Jewish Condition

Rabbi Lawrence A. Hoffman, PhD

Rabbi Lawrence A. Hoffman, PhD, is the Barbara and Stephen Friedman Professor of Liturgy, Worship and Ritual at the Hebrew Union
College–Jewish Institute of Religion in New York. In 1995, he co-
founded Synagogue 2000, dedicated to transforming synagogues into
spiritual and moral centers for the twenty-first century. He has written or edited over forty books, including *Rethinking Synagogues* and
(co-edited) *Sacred Strategies: Transforming Synagogues from Functional to
Visionary*. He is the recipient of two National Jewish Book Awards, two
honorary doctorates, the Abraham Geiger Medal (from the Abraham
Geiger Rabbinic School in Berlin), and the *Berakah* Award for lifetime
achievement (from the North American Academy of Liturgy). He is a
regular speaker, lecturer, and consultant for synagogues worldwide.

Leadership has always mattered to Jews. It is hard to imagine
how we managed to get from Egypt to the Land of Israel without it, and the witticism "From Moses to Moses, there was no one
like Moses"—used variously to refer to Moses Maimonides (1135–
1204), Moses Mendelssohn (1729–1786), and Moses Montefiore
(1784–1885)—attests not just to the redundancy of Judaism's favorite name but to the Jewish focus on leaders. Yet traditional Jewish
study has remained remarkably unaware of leadership as a subject
worthy of serious study.

The same could be said of Western culture generally. Despite clear treatments of leadership running all the way back through Max Weber, Machiavelli, and Plato, it was not until the late twentieth century that both leadership studies and leadership development came into their own. Whether or not Peter Drucker was correct when he recalled, in 2004, that he was "the first one to talk about leadership, 50 years ago,"[1] he was certainly not wrong in identifying leadership as a field that had barely been born back then. Warren Bennis's classic *On Becoming a Leader* came out only in 1989—just four years after his self-professed first publication on the subject (*Leaders*, co-authored with Burt Nanus), which, he says, made him "suddenly ... a ranking authority."[2] Similar pioneers in the field (some of them represented in this book), such as Bernard Bass, James MacGregor Burns, Ronald Heifetz, and Barbara Kellerman, for example, began writing about leadership then as well.

By now, however, leadership has emerged as the quintessential worry of our time—the way social work, as a discipline (and social action as a religious imperative), became important around the turn of the twentieth century, when (to quote Emma Lazarus's poem, now engraved on the Statue of Liberty) "huddled masses" from eastern and southern Europe began swamping American shores. What social work was then, leadership is now—still a relatively new topic, but a burgeoning one, constituting the core of what Barbara Kellerman (a contributor here) has called a veritable "leadership industry."[3]

There is as yet nothing close to a *Jewish* leadership industry, however; specifically "Jewish" attention to the subject is at best episodic. But as interest in leadership mounts everywhere, increasing numbers of Jews want to know how leadership in general intersects with Judaism in particular.

This book explores that intersection, by assembling (for the very first time) the requisite experts on both sides of the equation—leadership studies, on one hand, and Jewish studies, on the other—and it juxtaposes academicians who study leadership with leading rabbis, professionals, and volunteers who practice it.

That this marriage of theory and practice has occurred at all is the result of the single most prominent voice promoting it: Leslie

Wexner. The Wexner Foundation, chaired by Les and his wife, Abigail, has conscientiously furthered its founder's realization some thirty years ago that seriousness about leadership was the "unmet need" of the time. To meet the need, the foundation adopted a series of initiatives to root leadership deeply in Jewish consciousness. It crisscrossed major cities in North America to identify lay leaders in the making and treat them to serious and ongoing two-year-long courses in Jewish studies and leadership competence. It awarded fellowships to promising young professionals, supplementing their professional training with leadership enrichment. And it brought young and talented civil servants from Israel to study leadership at Harvard's John F. Kennedy School of Government. In 2015, some thirteen hundred of the faculty, alumni, and students indebted to the Wexners' foresight and investment descended upon their hometown of Columbus, Ohio, to celebrate the foundation's thirty-year anniversary.

This book follows upon that celebration. It assembles, for the very first time, some fifty contributions on leadership, by an assortment of scholars and practitioners who have been central to the Wexner project: faculty from the Kennedy School; Israelis who have studied there and are now applying what they learned to initiatives back home; internationally known writers and thinkers from the disciplines that constitute Jewish studies; and selected Wexner fellows and communal leaders (lay and professional) for whom Jewish leadership has become a necessary part of their evolving work throughout North America.

This remarkable mix is testimony to the thirty years of leadership exercised by Leslie Wexner himself, but it is no mere encomium to him. Rather, it makes its own contribution to the field of leadership, by combining leadership studies with Jewish studies (the Bible, Jewish law, Jewish history, and so on), to understand leadership in all its Jewish specificity. Contributions are short and accessible, the sort of thing that boards of directors, professional staffs, rabbis, executive directors, and volunteers everywhere will find most worthwhile.

The book begins, appropriately, with contributions from experts in both fields (leadership and Jewish studies), entitled

"What Leaders Need to Know": first, "Lessons on Leadership" generally; and then, "Jewish Models of Leadership" specifically.

The "general lessons" include synopses of classic concepts that leaders are widely assumed by now to know, as well as novel insights still growing in importance, the next frontier into leadership for our time. In short order, readers learn such things as the following:

- Innovation and adaptability as components of Jewish history (Ronald Heifetz)
- The difference between leadership and management (Wexner Foundation's senior philanthropic adviser, Larry Moses); and first principles and mission (Dr. David T. Ellwood)
- The technique of nudging (Dr. Max H. Bazerman)
- The art of inclusion (Patricia Bellinger)
- The role of authenticity (Harvard senior fellow Bill George)
- The attention we must pay to actual leaders—how "Hitler's ghost" still haunts us (Dr. Barbara Kellerman)
- Measures of effective teamwork (Rabbi Aaron Panken, PhD)
- Principles of negotiation (Dr. Brian Mandell)
- Risk readiness (Arna Poupko Fisher)
- The challenge of constant change (Marty Linsky)
- Lessons in leadership from "The Court of St. James's" (Ambassador Daniel Taub)
- The importance of "presence" (Rae Ringel)
- The importance even of our own moods ("the mood elevator" —Dr. Larry Senn)

These general lessons synopsize classic literature on leadership and are applied here by many of the very authors who pioneered the lessons in question. But their application overlaps with the section following, "Jewish Models of Leadership." We see (in the first section), for example, how Ronald Heifetz's distinction between technical problems and adaptive challenges applies to the Bible and the Rabbis. This second section continues the overlap but in the other direction: it highlights specifically *Jewish* leadership paradigms, through explorations of Jewish law and history—in the

Bible, Talmudic tradition, and beyond. Metaphors and models run delightfully wild here as authors mine the whole of Jewish life and lore for colorful characterizations of the way Judaism understands leadership: "Leading from Tents, Not from Arks" (Rabbi Joanna Samuels), "The Global Wrap of T'fillin" (Rabbi Asher Lopatin), and "Marshmallows, Ketchup, and Redemption" (Rabbi Jacob J. Schacter, PhD). The voices are many and diverse in this closing unit of part one, as rabbis, professors, business leaders, volunteers, and professionals provide moving examples of the many ways that Jewish learning and identity motivate their personal leadership stance.

But the focus of our book is twofold: not just the practice of leadership, but the state of affairs in which Jewish communities find themselves—the area, that is, where this leadership must be exercised. Part one, "What Leaders Need to Know," is therefore followed by part two, "The Jewish Condition," a set of snapshot-like profiles of Jewish life and the leadership required for it to prosper. The contributions break down easily into three categories: lessons applicable everywhere—"The Global View," that is; then "Challenges in Israel" and "Challenges in America," specifically. In all three cases, readers will be struck by the honesty with which the authors approach their analyses. Authors obeyed their mandate to write briefly and accessibly, but also insightfully and incisively—to provide, in short, what we need to know about the problems and challenges to which leaders need be responsive.

Typical of the global view are Rabbi Irving (Yitz) Greenberg's celebrated theory of "Three Eras of Jewish History and Their Leaders"; Dr. Robert Chazan's historical summary of "Why Programs in Leadership? Why Now?" and Dr. Deborah E. Lipstadt's recollection of the way Jewish leaders coalesced to rebut the calumnies of Holocaust deniers ("The Jewish People's Story, Not Just My Own").

The examples from Israel will prove especially instructive to North American readers who get a great deal of "bird's-eye" reportage on Israel, but relatively little about the details of Israeli life "on the ground"—such things as the following:

- Battling corruption in a diverse democracy (Avia Alef, Adv, LLM, MC-MPA)
- Speaking up for Israel's voiceless (Sharon Abraham-Weiss, Adv, LLM, MC-MPA)
- An approach to disabled children (Dr. Maurit Beeri)
- Promoting gender equality in Israel's celebrated Defense Forces, the IDF (Brigadier General Rachel Tevet Wiesel)
- The enduring model, even today, of Israel's founding prime minister, David Ben-Gurion (Major General [retired] Amos Yadlin)

As for North America, we get a broad selection of issues, described by experts working with them—everything from the feminist struggle within Orthodox Judaism (Dr. Sharon Weiss-Greenberg) to the need for moral leadership in the running of Jewish day schools (Rabbi Judd Kruger Levingston, PhD).

The book is bracketed by an introduction and conclusion that are stellar examples of leadership in their own right. Rabbi B. Elka Abrahamson, president of The Wexner Foundation, provides her insider's view of the leadership principles practiced in the foundation. Leslie Wexner himself concludes with a recollection of how he turned to leadership to begin with and some of the leadership insights that have guided his forays into business and philanthropy. We introduce this Wexner essay with creative contributions by noted political analyst, White House adviser, and professor David Gergen and by Charles R. Bronfman, philanthropist, friend, and colleague of Leslie Wexner over the years.

As several of the essays indicate, the need for leadership is hardly novel; it goes back as far as memory reaches. But only now are we addressing leadership—and Jewish leadership at that—with all due intentionality. This book breaks new ground in that regard. It combines leadership studies in general with the Jewish perspective on leadership in particular, and it surveys not just leadership as the growing field that it is, but the Jewish condition midway into the second decade of the twenty-first century—a case study in its own right of how attention to leadership is changing the world in which we live.

A Values Map
The Journey to Our Best Selves

Rabbi B. Elka Abrahamson

Rabbi B. Elka Abrahamson is president of The Wexner Foundation. She oversees the foundation's full range of activities and, in partnership with foundation chairmen Abigail and Leslie Wexner, imagines how the foundation might further strengthen and educate Jewish professional and volunteer leaders in North America and public service leaders in the State of Israel. A pulpit rabbi and informal Jewish educator for more than fifteen years prior to her work at Wexner, Rabbi Abrahamson is a sought-after teacher and speaker. She is optimistic about the Jewish future owing to the remarkable leaders she encounters in her rabbinate, many of them Wexner alumni.

Familiar as it may be, it is a leadership story worth repeating:

> The great Hasidic leader Zusya approached his followers, his eyes red with tears, his face pale with fear.
>
> "Zusya, what's the matter? You look frightened!"
>
> "The other day, I had a vision. In it, *I learned the question that the angels will one day ask me about my life.*"
>
> The followers were puzzled. "Zusya, you are a good person, caring, responsible and loving. What final question could terrify you so?"

Zusya gazed heavenward. "I learned that the angels will not ask me, 'Why weren't you a Moses, leading your people out of slavery, or a Miriam, leading your people in a dance of redemption?' Rather, they will ask, 'Zusya, why weren't you Zusya?'"

This is *the* question to which leaders must return again and again: Who are you? Embedded in it are more focused questions on which leadership depends:

- Am I mindful of how I myself am evolving as a leader and a person?
- What is the gap between where I am now and where I ought to be?
- Toward what am I exercising leadership?
- Where will I take my organization? My community? Where am I taking myself?
- What is the path from here to there?

These demanding questions emerge from the Zusya story because they represent a rigorous self-assessment and because they presuppose honesty at the very core of who we are. These questions receive no final answers—the answers necessarily change with time, for the world changes and so do we. Effective leaders are called upon to guide others through those changes. Indeed, at The Wexner Foundation, we believe that leadership is fundamentally about managing change.

Perhaps, what The Wexner Foundation does best is provide the space, the cohort, and the guidance to navigate these personally demanding prompts. Toward that end, we have developed seven core values, honed over many years and tested regularly throughout our organization. We hold one another responsible to them. They are our North Star, our way to become our own authentic "Zusya"—the person we are meant to be—that we might build an organization of excellence: reflective, disciplined, purposed, and energized by clear expectations.

1. **We embrace Jewish diversity.** We model pluralist Jewish community, fostering a steadfast respect for difference and

serving the many different expressions of Jewish life with uniform sincerity. In pursuit of pluralism we intentionally select groups that bring together individuals of vastly different backgrounds, denominations, and practices. We devise thoughtfully outlined rules of engagement to enable civil discourse across serious differences. We ask that participants give one another the benefit of the doubt as to their sincerity and integrity.

Here lies the baseline of dialogue across difference, a climate increasingly rare in contemporary conversation. Steadfast mutual respect is the bedrock upon which effective and enduring leadership teams are built. Such teams encourage understanding, not consensus; and expect that individuals will talk to, rather than at, one another.

2. **We value emotional intelligence.** Emotional intelligence is the ongoing intentional effort to be self-aware, to master reflective practice, and to demonstrate the capacity to listen. Emotionally intelligent leaders remain ever conscious of their fears, biases, and vulnerabilities. They take the time to perceive the mood of others, to take others seriously, and to respond thoughtfully and honestly to what others bring to the table.

3. **We practice patience.** The Hebrew root of the word for "patience," *savlanut (s.v.l.)*, can also mean "to bear or suffer through." Patience is the ability to bear the inevitable discomfort of change and to engage with those who disagree—a particularly rigorous strain on leaders. Patience strengthens the spiritual muscles and emotional flexibility required to carry the load of complicated conversation and negative feedback—and to treat these as part of the process rather than a mere burden. Patience prevents our crumbling under the weight of disagreement, discouragement, and inconvenience. Ultimately, it strengthens us.

4. **We operate with agility and optimism.** The pace of organizational change can be painfully slow. Energizing a community in the face of the inevitability of organizational entropy

and the complacency and apathy that it causes is no easy matter. The effort can easily erode a leader's enthusiasm and confidence precisely when the people we seek to inspire require just the reverse.

Agility is the capacity to switch gears, handle surprises, and adopt new strategies, particularly when the path we are on is merely draining our energy and getting us nowhere. It seeks solutions on the margins, not just the mainstream, and demands that we be as wary of writing off the new as we normally are about jettisoning the old. Agility recharges the batteries of enthusiasm.

5. **We cultivate creativity and curiosity.** Our chairman, Leslie Wexner, is a profile in curiosity and a master of imagination. He, and we, admire a teaching attributed to Albert Einstein: curiosity is more important than knowledge. Curious leaders are always learning, experimenting, and pushing one another to go beyond the obvious. They seek new patterns that predict what is around that next corner. Plenty of smart people fail to knock on the door of their own ingenuity, forget how to color outside the lines, and succumb to the current of organizational habit. They fall into the rut of "what is" at the expense of imagining "what if?"

6. **We treasure humor.** Leadership, though serious, should be fun. Play, it turns out, is the most creative human mode of all. It makes leadership uplifting and good for the *neshamah*—the spirit and the soul. Laughing at oneself signals permission for others to do the same. Laughter fuels our energy.

7. **We strive for humility.** Humility of heart is the gateway to openness. It enables leaders to measure the amount of space they are taking up in the room—and then to step back and draw others in. It permits us to embrace our shortcomings and identify our blind spots. It paves the way for respectful listening and signals a willingness to collaborate—a core requirement for exercising effective leadership.

These are the values that drive us and that we teach. Each person, certainly each leader, will add their own. How are those values reflected in the behaviors and outcomes of whatever it is that you lead? What values map your leadership journey? Naming and living by them is a compass guiding you to your best self. No power of heaven or earth should prevent you from that. What is the path from here to there—the path to becoming your own best Zusya?

PART ONE

What Leaders Need to Know

▲

Lessons on Leadership

Nudging as a Tool of Leaders

Dr. Max H. Bazerman

Dr. Max H. Bazerman is Jesse Isidor Straus Professor of Business Administration at the Harvard Business School and the co-director of the Center for Public Leadership at Harvard's John F. Kennedy School of Government. He is the author, co-author, or co-editor of twenty books, including *The Power of Noticing* and *Blind Spots* (with Ann Tenbrunsel), and over two hundred research articles and chapters. His awards include an honorary doctorate from the University of London (London Business School) and both the Distinguished Educator Award and the Distinguished Scholar Award from the Academy of Management. His external work involves teaching and consulting in thirty countries. More details are available at www.people.hbs.edu /mbazerman.

In 2014, the Israeli minister of health began requiring citizens seeking a new or renewed ID card, passport, or driver's license to answer the question of whether they would register as an organ donor. "No" was an acceptable answer; not answering was not. This process, which roughly matches those in place in the United Kingdom and other countries, dramatically increases the number of organ donations by getting citizens to at least think about the issue. The policy also addresses the concern of critics who argue that putting people in the organ-donation system automatically, and requiring them to take some action to opt out, is manipulative and potentially in violation of religious preferences. This new policy required an act of leadership, and it will save lives!

This change in Israeli law is consistent with a new wave of leadership tools sweeping governments around the globe: *nudges*. If, for example, you wanted to encourage people to be truthful when filling out a tax return, would it make more sense to

a) have them fill out the form, and sign at the end, attesting that the information is accurate, or

b) sign a statement first, attesting that the information that they are about to provide is true?

Most leaders to whom I pose this question select the second option as more effective, and my research with Lisa Shu, Nina Mazar, Francesca Gino, and Dan Ariely confirms they are right.[1] Why, then, have we been getting it wrong for so long? This evidence of how leaders can nudge people toward honesty is reforming how governments collect fees and taxes. A host of such insights will almost certainly become part of the leadership toolkit over the upcoming years.

The books *Nudge* by Richard H. Thaler and Cass R. Sunstein and *Thinking, Fast and Slow* by Daniel Kahneman highlight how behavioral economics and other behavioral sciences shed light on our decision-making processes.[2] The United Kingdom's Behavioural Insights Team has demonstrated an ability to save dollars and lives, put students in the classroom, and get people to act in healthier ways. These insights do much more than improve how individuals make important personal decisions. They help leaders make better decisions about policies that impact society. The basic idea is that through a better understanding of human cognition, we can create "choice architecture" that is more likely to produce wise decisions for the decision maker and the broader society.

I have the good fortune to be the co-director, with David Gergen, of the Center for Public Leadership (CPL) at the Harvard Kennedy School of Government. CPL is the direct result of the vision of Leslie and Abigail Wexner. CPL seeks to identify new concepts and strategies for the next generation of leaders. Within CPL, Iris Bohnet and I co-chair the Behavioral Insights Group (BIG). Launched in 2013, BIG brings together Harvard's outstanding group of decision research scholars, behavioral economists, and other behavioral scientists to focus their energies on improving how decisions are made, both by leaders and by individuals. BIG is driven by the belief that improving the quality of our leaders' decisions is a core lever we possess to improving the world.

When leaders and individuals make better decisions, an amazing array of changes can improve everything from education and health care to the environment; it reduces discrimination and enhances personal financial decisions. Thaler and Sunstein document the amazing effectiveness of nudging to increase the likelihood of employees saving for retirement. They show that if a firm wants its employees to save, rather than requiring employees to fill out a form to start the saving, firms can enroll employees automatically in a retirement savings account and allow them to opt out if they do not want to be in the plan. Again, the improvement is surprisingly large.

As a research program hosted by the CPL and the Harvard Kennedy School, BIG integrates its research with the teaching and social change initiatives of the center and the school. A key outcome for BIG is teaching Harvard Kennedy School students in degree programs, executive education, and other seminars and workshops how to use behavioral insights to become more effective change agents and to improve the state of organizations, policy, and the world.

In the 2014–2015 academic year, Professor Michael Luca and I co-taught a course entitled "UK and the Netherlands: Behavioral Insights." The course featured six two-hour class sessions over the fall semester on the subject of behavioral science and public policy. It partnered thirty-seven students with ten clients (specifically, government agencies) in the United Kingdom and the Netherlands with whom they worked on specific projects related to behavioral science applications to policy. Students worked with actual clients seeking genuine solutions to agency problems by using psychological insights. By thinking about small but powerful changes that were likely to be embraced and applied by their clients, and adapting to unexpected challenges, the students gained the tools they will need to apply insights from behavioral science to their own work and organizations.

We have also made considerable progress in connecting with emerging behavioral insight teams around the globe, including in the United Kingdom, Singapore, Israel, Australia, the Netherlands, and a number of countries that are just beginning to create units in this area of leadership skills. The growth is enormous. After launching the BIG entity, our students worked with us to create the Behavioral Insights Study Group, a self-managed community of over seven hundred graduate students that will enhance our ability to bring this work to our students.

Most views of leadership focus on changing the hearts and minds of followers. Nudging often skips hearts and minds to directly change behavior through choice architecture without people even knowing they have been nudged. I do not view nudges as an alternative to other leadership insights. Rather, I see the use of behavioral insights as a new set of tools that should be a part of the skillset of all leaders.

The Power of Inclusion

PATRICIA BELLINGER

Patricia Bellinger is executive director of the Center for Public Leadership and an adjunct lecturer at Harvard's John F. Kennedy School of Government. She is a sought-after speaker, worldwide, for her expertise on diversity and inclusion in organizations. In addition to her work at the Center, Patricia teaches inclusive leadership within the degree program, for the Kennedy School's offerings in executive education, and for the Center's leadership development programming. Following an extensive private sector career, she serves on several boards including Sodexo S.A. and Pattern Energy. Patricia and her husband, Richard Balzer, are the proud parents of four children.

Throughout my career, I have focused on the power of inclusion as the best way to foster and lead successful organizations. I have been witness to and experienced the impact of exclusion. I have also been encouraged, enlightened, and inspired by its opposite. Inclusive leadership taps into the broadest pool of talent, unleashes skills and passions, and creates deep wells of engagement and loyalty among teams. Leading inclusively also has the moral underpinning of a simple truth: lead others as you would wish to be led. Everything I know, have learned, teach—and indeed, am—has forged my belief in the power of inclusion.

When I was in eighth grade, my parents and I decided that I should switch from a solid public school to a private, Catholic, all-girls school even though we are not a Catholic family, and I would be one of three African American girls in the student body of four

9

hundred. Despite my excellent academic record, school administrators, who presumed me incapable of handling upper-level math and science, planned to place me in lower-level classes, to "protect me" from failure. My parents insisted I would do just fine in the higher-level classes, and I did—becoming one of the first two students from that school to head to an Ivy League institution upon graduation. That lack of inclusion—the feeling that the system I was in did not believe in and support me—was a significant burden for the young girl I was then.

Mahzarin Banaji and Tony Greenwald have documented the pervasive presence of implicit bias in our society and the fact that all human beings, to varying degrees, have and act on implicit biases. These biases remain unaddressed for the simple reason that "their possessors are unaware of possessing them."[1] The authors suggest a way for "good people to align intentions with their behavior."[2]

Implicit biases limit our views about where and how to locate the most talented individuals, and the appearance, demeanor, education, racial, ethnic, and religious background of who those individuals "probably are." Inclusive leaders reach beyond the usual suspects and places to find and hire the best.

One of the most interesting and innovative approaches to this issue is the technique of *blind auditions*, a practice that eliminates implicit gender bias and increases the gender diversity of musicians in orchestras worldwide.[3] A firm called GapJumpers has brought the approach to scale, enabling organizations to evaluate talent based on performance challenges rather than on "pre-conceived notions of what talent looks like and where it comes from."[4] The multipronged approaches these authors recommend are effortful, but worth it. An African proverb advises, "If you wish to move a mountain tomorrow, you must start by lifting stones today."

Every leader wants to create an organizational culture in which her teams do their best work and feel motivated to go above and beyond. Most leaders value low turnover and high staff engagement as sure signs of success but do not realize the extent to which these goals can be furthered by a leader's focus on inclusion. Among the most important works on the subject is the research of

Kenji Yoshino and Christie Smith, who explain why diversity and inclusion efforts remain stalled, twenty years out.[5] They identify what I believe to be the key to an inclusive environment: one's ability to bring one's authentic self to work. Their thesis is that "most inclusion efforts have not explicitly and rigorously addressed the pressure to conform that most workplaces exert ... despite stating inclusion as one of their core institutional values."[6] In their study across industries involving thousands of respondents, 53 percent said their leaders expect them to cover up core aspects of their identity at work! As to the impact of this expectation, at least 50 percent reported a diminished sense of opportunities available to them and lower commitment to the organization as a result.[7]

Most of us have experienced exclusion at one time or another in our lives; it can be debilitating, sometimes paralyzing, and detrimental to one's mental (and sometimes physical) well-being. How often have we regretted our own failure to include someone who has been overlooked, someone more reserved, undervalued, and often "different"? The harm is done to that individual, but the loss is our own as well. True leaders set the cultural tone and determine who is recognized and rewarded and why. They have the power to bring everyone in from the cold, closer to the flame at the organizational center, to lead the way to greater inclusion, fulfillment, and better results.

Perhaps my most powerful experience of inclusive leadership occurred upon my arrival as a senior executive at BP, an organization that in the year 2000 could fairly be described as male-dominated, unreconstructed, British American, and white. My ostensible boss was a senior human resources leader, but my mentor and sponsor was the deputy CEO of BP as a whole. As a leader he was deeply respected, somewhat feared, and greatly admired. His first act of inclusion was to dedicate considerable time each day to meet with me, get to know me, and teach me about the company, the industry, and leadership. I learned a great deal from these meetings, but the bigger story was that just by spending so much time with me, he was sending powerful signals about the importance of my new role and his commitment to my success.

On the top executive floor where he held court in his corner suite, all the offices were glass-fronted. By the end of the second week, every executive on the floor went from wondering who I was to seeking out meetings with me. During my meetings with the deputy CEO, he called all of the most important divisional leaders around the world and instructed them that I would be traveling to interview them about their leadership and organizations. His tone and message conveyed the expectation that they would take me seriously, answer my questions, share information, and hide nothing. By the time the next senior leadership conference rolled around, I knew half the people in the room and had their attention. My task was to lead the organization on a journey of diversity and inclusion. My mentor gave me a subtle yet powerful master class in the art of inclusion, which I have not forgotten.

▲▾▲▾▲▾▲▾▲▾▲▾▲▾▲▾▲

Purpose, People, and Principle

Leadership for the Unnatural Leader

DR. DAVID T. ELLWOOD

Dr. David T. Ellwood is the Scott M. Black Professor of Political Economy at Harvard's John F. Kennedy School of Government. He was dean of the school from 2004 to 2015. A labor economist whose work centers on poverty, families, and social policy, Dr. Ellwood has significantly influenced public policy in the United States and abroad. In 1993, he was named assistant secretary for planning and evaluation at the U.S. Department of Health and Human Services, where he co-chaired President Clinton's Working Group on Welfare Reform, Family Support and Independence. He currently chairs the U.S. Partnership on Mobility from Poverty, a group of twenty-four leading scholars and practitioners, supported by the Gates Foundation, who are charged with crafting "big bets" to dramatically increase upward mobility of the poor.

I was the nerdy guy in high school who carried a briefcase. A friend once said, "Even if you were the best tennis player in the school, the team wouldn't elect you captain." Yet I somehow had the honor and pleasure to lead the Harvard Kennedy School (a school of government and public service) for nearly a dozen years. Unsurprisingly, I am squarely in the "leadership can be learned" camp.

Here, then, are the personal reflections of someone not born to lead, who nonetheless loved leading. These are a work in progress; insights often taken from counselors wiser than I; maxims I gradually adopted as I led an institution with high aspirations.

The first and most essential part of my becoming a credible leader was to ...

Seize a Mission of Purpose

As I looked for ways to convey aspirations of a mission-driven organization, I turned to my thesaurus, seeking synonyms for "idealism." The first two words I found were "naiveté" and "romanticism." Naively and romantically, then, I believe that leaders and institutions that effectively evoke idealism have an amazing, almost unfair advantage. The combination of ideals and ideas can bind together disparate people and groups better than economic or personal self-interest ever will. And when devoted people work together, magic happens.

A "mission of purpose" should reflect the core values of the organization—for the Kennedy School, that is to make the world a better place. Really. Throughout my deanship I incessantly repeated that mission in virtually every meeting, every speech. You might think it trite or stale, yet for eleven years, insiders and outsiders alike accepted it as the invitation to make a difference in society, a contribution bigger than our individual interests. Whenever we focused on making the world a better place, the discussion was better, the decision felt right, hurt feelings were diminished, and our sense of community was enhanced.

Such an overarching mission of purpose is vulnerable to seeming commonplace or meaningless, unless one regularly reinforces, redefines, celebrates, and animates it. Moreover, a mission that is grandiose and all-encompassing requires clarity of focus. The institution must commit itself to specific people and projects that "walk the walk" and demonstrate the institution's bottom-line purpose.

Those choices require colleagues with rich and diverse wisdom. Which is why ...

It Takes a Portfolio of People

People seem drawn to the forceful, hyper-confident leader who always seems to know what to do and where we need to go. The media celebrate generals, presidents, and CEOs who, through resolve, insight, and personality, won the war, transformed the nation, or created an industry. That's fine for Teddy Roosevelt, Nelson Mandela, or Steve Jobs, but what about the rest of us?

I once thought my job was to tell people what they should do and how to do it—that's a lonely and barren road to travel. Fortunately, I found it more effective and creative to hire and support terrific people who were good at the very things I was not. My role was mostly figuring out, with them, what they needed to be wildly successful.

We are normally attracted to people most like ourselves, whereas what we need is people with different insights, skills, and sensibilities, people who will challenge us and one another, even as they work together. Such diverse and dynamic people do not naturally form a cohesive team. Some thrive on conflict; others fear it. Some share; some horde. Some value independence; others want the thrill of working together on all key decisions. This diversity can be welded together only by a shared sense of mission. Leaders can give people the different things they need while insisting that they work as a unit, being loyal to the institution whose cause they all champion.

I learned from Leslie Wexner, "The leader defines the tone of the whole organization." Every organization has a feel, a culture that establishes how people are treated and what they aspire to. Some places are demanding and competitive; others practice generosity and nurturing. Either style can succeed or fail. Still, for organizations with a purpose-driven mission, my bias is a culture that treats people with the dignity and respect that seems inherent in their mission—*so long as* the organization also expects and celebrates superior performance.

With even the best people, though, there will still be crises; and that is when one needs to ...

Define and Defend First Principles

Let's play a quick game of "You Are the Dean."

A faculty member, staffer, student, or internal group has earnestly championed some position that others find flawed, offensive, even dangerous. Outraged objectors demand that the school condemn the words and discipline the "culprits." Their case seems strong; the hurt very real; your in-box is bombarded; social media are in an uproar. What do you do?

"Crisis Management 101" recommends rapid evaluation of the organization's interests and risks, followed by decisive expressions of concern, a promise of internal reforms, and action to prevent such incidents in the future.

One of the most important and painful lessons I learned at the Kennedy School is that really serious crises are often existential threats. More than clever political wordsmithing or creative one-off strategies, they require turning to first principles. Universities are one of the few places left where ideas can openly compete on their merits, not the power of their constituencies. Universities cradle the firm belief in the capacity of educated human beings to listen to evidence and argument so that good ideas drive out the bad.

Yet universities often fail to live up to these ideals. If educational leaders too easily condemn and censor ideas, even those we consider deeply flawed, do we not run the risk of creating a climate so sterile, so resistant to controversy, so dependent on appeasement, that we become just another political battleground, rather than a haven of reflection, dialogue, innovation, and transformation?

First principles are not really the same as mission. Mission is aspirational; first principles are the core of your soul. They establish what is most fundamental, but that does not make them an invincible shield. I have almost never convinced anyone outraged or hurt by a particular speaker, paper, or academic activity that a principle of open debate and dialogue was more important than having the institution publicly reject the notion they find so dangerous or offensive. Still, many eventually believed I actually was standing on principle, and that helped, inside and out.

I am not trying to generalize this particular core principle to other organizations; some educational leaders would disagree with me even about its centrality to education. My point, rather, is that first principles must guide decisions on where and when to take a stand, even an unpopular and potentially job-threatening stand.

That's it. I fear my maxims offer rather thin gruel: a mission of purpose, a portfolio of people, and first principles. No wonder I never became tennis captain. Still these basic guideposts have let me spend more than a decade learning, sharing, nurturing, and leading at what I found to be the best job in the whole world.

Leading So You Get It Wrong

Arna Poupko Fisher

Arna Poupko Fisher earned her degree in medieval Jewish philosophy from Yeshiva University, continued graduate work in the philosophy of halachah at McGill University, and now teaches Bible and Jewish thought in the Judaic Studies Department of the University of Cincinnati. While in Montreal, she was the first to serve as a full-time "scholar in residence" for a Federation—groundbreaking work that was recognized by the Avi Chai Foundation. Since then, she has lectured and taught in over 130 Jewish communities, on Jewish thought, Jewish law, leadership, and ethics. She has been a core faculty member of the Wexner Heritage Program since 1998, is on the Executive Committee of the Cincinnati Federation, and serves as a trustee on the Jewish Foundation of Cincinnati.

My dad was a serial empiricist, a professor of engineering who approached life's questions with the simple formula "What do we know and how do we know it?" I was comforted by the knowledge that Dad's logical and unbiased judgment would arrive at the answers to all things.

> "The totality of true thoughts is a picture of the world."
>
> —Ludwig Wittgenstein[1]

But Dad was also a serial inventor. At ten, he had built an automatic wagon made out of spare washing machine parts, and as an adult (long before it was fashionable), he explored wind, ice, and solar power. My dad's side of the garage was a repository of hybrid contraptions/vehicles/machines, all of them products of his bold imagination and entrepreneurial spirit.

> "Logic, he [Wittgenstein] says, pervades the world: the boundaries of the world are also its boundaries."
> —BERTRAND RUSSELL[2]

The pinnacle of these wacky inventions was his "flying boat," a way for non-pilots to experience the miraculous sensation of flight. He was a pilot himself, but also a sailor, two passions that inspired his Hydro Plane, a speedboat with an extended arm that allowed its rider, belted in a harness, to be suspended twelve feet above the water and steer the boat with a right/left, up/down mechanism, as if one were in an open-air cockpit. It was a wondrous and terrifying thing—but it was difficult to find test pilots.

> "In the proposition, therefore, its sense is not yet contained, but the possibility of expressing it."
> —LUDWIG WITTGENSTEIN[3]

When it finally debuted, at the 2005 Vancouver International Boat Show, bewildered boat aficionados dutifully accepted brochures from the polite, professorial, eighty-five-year-old gentleman in the captain's hat. When the project proved a "bust," Dad remained content and even bemused—the logical engineer committed to singularly truthful propositions about all things, but equally at home in the dualities of certainty and ambiguity; the empiricist, with total faith in math and science, but thoroughly comfortable in the unknown outcomes of madcap inventions and the reality of human vulnerability and likely failure. He was able to thrive, confidently and deliberately, in the world of absolute doubt.

> "The world and life are one."
> —LUDWIG WITTGENSTEIN[4]

Our inclination, as leaders, is to feel that we are perfect and to be drawn to organizations and initiatives that most seamlessly reinforce the effectiveness of our skills and the positive sense of our own success. We seek out volunteers and colleagues who share our concerns, strategies, and visions and who build together with us a community of comfortable like-mindedness. My dad, by contrast, embraced the uncomfortable but emotional richness that accompanies risk, even ineptitude.

Leaders who seek transformation and originality must be willing to put themselves at personal risk. Leaders who are fearful of failure will never manage to negotiate the rough terrain of communal disagreement, without seeing the "other side" as anathema. They will never stretch the fearful possibly of being wrong into a welcome opportunity for growth.

> "In logic, therefore, we cannot say, 'There is this and this in the world, but not that,' for to say so would apparently presuppose that we exclude certain possibilities, and this cannot be the case, since it would require that logic should go beyond the boundaries of the world, as if it could contemplate these boundaries from the other side also."
>
> —BERTRAND RUSSELL[5]

The more leaders perceive their personal reputations and even legacies to be at stake, the more risk-averse and protective they can become. But as my father demonstrated, this is precisely the time to embrace the role of being the one to know the least, to fumble as the novice chairman, or to simply "get it wrong."

My father's most humiliating invention was the "rocket"-fueled ice glider, scheduled to make its debut between periods of a sold-out Edmonton Oiler's hockey game. The test driver was a student my father tapped from the philosophy department because, he said, "in the event that something goes terribly wrong, better to not lose a student devoted to an empirical science." After a highly energetic introduction of "the professor and his futuristic groundbreaking rocket sled," my dad ignited the metal tube that extended from the back of the sled, and with fire blazing like a rocket headed to the moon, it sped out onto the ice only to stop, abruptly and inexplicably, just short of the blue line. As my dad retrieved the contraption and its shaken Hegelian driver, the arena went dead silent—and then erupted in boos and jeers, with one unforgettable heckler shouting, "Why don't you just wind it up, Mack?"

Standing on the sidelines, I realized that in addition to everything else that had gone wrong, I had failed to execute the one simple task I had been given: to clock the time it took the rocket sled to circle the arena. As the professor and the student hobbled off the ice, I held up the stopwatch and said meekly, "Dad, I forgot." He looked at me, with the contented smile of a soul who saw defeat as an opportunity for the next round of discovery, and said sweetly, "Arna, that's the least of our problems."

True leaders are brave, confident, and humble enough to smile expectantly when they get it wrong.

> "My propositions are elucidatory in this way: he who understands finally recognizes them as senseless as if he has climbed out through them, over them, on them, and thrown away the ladder after he has climbed up on it; then he sees the world rightly."
> —Ludwig Wittgenstein[6]

My father, Professor David Panar, taught mechanical engineering at the University of Michigan and returned to his native Canada, where he continued to teach and practice. With his tenure pending, he left to volunteer in the MACHAL unit (volunteers from outside of Israel) during the War of Independence. He, along with a few others, successfully built the first Israeli military plane, known as "the Black Split." It was flown every Yom Ha'atzmaut (Israeli Independence Day) and now rests in the Beersheba Israel Air Force Museum.

The Epitome of an Authentic Leader

BILL GEORGE

Bill George is senior fellow at Harvard Business School, where he has taught leadership since 2004. His four best-selling books include, most recently, *Discover Your True North*. He was senior executive with Honeywell and Litton Industries and the former chairman and chief executive officer of Medtronic. He has served on many boards, including (currently) Goldman Sachs and the Mayo Clinic. His many honors include the Bower Award for Business Leadership (2014) and being named one of the "Top 25 Business Leaders of the Past 25 Years" (PBS), "Executive of the Year—2001" (the Academy of Management), and "Director of the Year—2001–02" (the National Association of Corporate Directors). He and his wife, Penny, reside in Minneapolis, Minnesota.

We have a crisis of confidence in our leaders, in business and in government. The latest Gallup poll shows that only 17 percent of those interviewed trust business leaders—not much higher than the miserable 8 percent rating of Congress. The failings of Wall Street bankers and the unethical dealings of formerly great companies like General Motors and Volkswagen have shaken public confidence in leaders to the core. Meanwhile, the systematic dismantling of corporate giants like DuPont and Kraft by activist hedge funds makes one wonder whether corporations have any purpose other than enhancing the net worth of the activists.

Despite these discouraging examples, however, I continue to believe that business is a noble calling. It holds the greatest hope for building our society, improving the quality of our lives, and rescuing people from poverty. It is the greatest wealth creator the world has ever known, and its opportunities are open to all, regardless of their station in life. Throughout my career I have tried to bring this clarity of purpose to leadership and encourage other leaders to do likewise.

After completing my career at Medtronic in 2002—where we were solely focused on restoring people to full health—I started taking a broader, and perhaps more objective, view of the wide range of business leaders in my generation and became deeply troubled by what I saw. Many of them seemed more focused on their own self-interest than on the interests of the organizations they led.

Often, their drive to succeed led them into unethical territory, as evidenced by the fall of Enron, WorldCom, and Tyco. In 2003, more than one hundred corporations made major earnings restatements to comply with the accounting standards of Sarbanes-Oxley, in order to avoid fraud charges. Just five years later, the short-term pressures of Wall Street resulted in the greatest financial collapse since the Great Depression and triggered the recession that followed.

In 2003, these concerns, alongside my thirty-three years of business experience, led me to write *Authentic Leadership*. It was my clarion call for a new kind of leader: the *authentic* leader, a leader able to fulfill the potential of business to serve society and improve quality of life around the world.

In the past thirteen years "authenticity" has emerged as the gold standard for leaders. Most of today's leaders have learned their lessons from the mistakes of my generation and are sincerely trying to lead with a clear purpose, practice their values, develop long-lasting relationships, build strong teams around them, and create value for all their constituencies—the characteristics of the authentic leaders I described back in 2003. As a result, the quality of today's leaders is far superior to those of my era, in spite of the few that have acted improperly.

Yet this unethical minority has created the current distrust of leaders generally, especially in business and politics, as if they all were solely out for themselves. The emergent leaders among the millennials (now becoming the majority, as they edge out aging baby boomers) need role models who have led authentically throughout their lifetimes. But who can they trust? Whom can they learn from?

Believing as I do that theory must be illustrated by real-life models, I offer Leslie Wexner as that role model, the epitome of an authentic leader.

Having known a wide array of leaders in business, I can say without overstatement that Leslie Wexner is *the gold standard* for authentic leadership. He knows what I call his "True North"—that is, he has clarity about the beliefs, values, and principles by which he leads. It didn't take a crisis for Les Wexner to get that way. It is simply *who he is*. Throughout his life he has followed his True North, as he built great retail enterprises and then gave back by becoming an equally great philanthropist. He has followed the adage "To whom much is given, much is expected."

For his entire career, Les has led with a deep sense of integrity—both his business and his personal life are beyond reproach. In large part, the authentic relationships he has developed with his colleagues, customers, employees, and investors hold the key to his sustained success. His fidelity to those relationships has garnered similar fidelity from others, in return, with the long-term consequence that he and his organizations have created value for all his constituencies and all who have worked with him.

In today's tumultuous times, where volatility, ambiguity, and uncertainty are the norm rather than the exception, leaders must have the capacity to adapt quickly to changes in markets and customers' preferences. In sharp contrast to retailers like Sears and K-Mart that failed to adjust to changes in consumers' preferences, Les has ensured his consumer offerings are "fashion forward" and ahead of the times. At the right moment, he had the wisdom to spin off retail offerings like Abercrombie & Fitch and Lane Bryant.

Devoted to developing authentic leaders, Les then created The Wexner Foundation to strengthen Jewish leadership, and more recently he expanded its mission to Catholic leadership as well. Among his most significant contributions are his $100 million donation to his alma mater, Ohio State, for the Wexner Medical Center. Now he is broadening his contributions to Harvard's Center for Public Leadership.

All this came about from humble origins. Les's parents were poor immigrants from Russia. From a $5,000 loan from his aunt in 1963, Les built his retail empire and a personal net worth that currently exceeds $8 billion. But he followed in the great Jewish tradition of *tikkun olam*, giving back to "better the world," and in that regard, Les is not alone. When examining the staggering contributions he has made through his philanthropy with his wife, Abigail, his business, and his service to America, one wonders where our country would be without the amazing generation of Jewish immigrants who came to this country before and after World War II.

I encourage today's emerging leaders to study Leslie Wexner's example of how to lead authentically, how to sustain leadership throughout your lifetime, and how to share the fruits of your labors with those who follow in your footprints. To paraphrase Henry Wadsworth Longfellow's "A Psalm of Life," leaders like Les Wexner leave "footprints on the sands of time." They become inspirations to us all.

Jewish Adaptability, Authority, and Leadership

Ronald Heifetz

Ronald Heifetz co-founded the Center for Public Leadership at Harvard's John F. Kennedy School of Government where he is the King Hussein bin Talal Senior Lecturer in Public Leadership. He speaks extensively and advises heads of governments, businesses, and non-profit organizations worldwide. His classic *Leadership without Easy Answers* (1994) is one of the ten most assigned course books at Harvard and Duke Universities. He coauthored (with Marty Linsky) the best-selling *Leadership on the Line* (2002); and (with Marty Linsky and Alexander Grashow) *The Practice of Adaptive Leadership* (2009). Heifetz's foundational course has consistently won the Alumni Award for the most influential course at the Kennedy School; his teaching methods are the subject of the book *Leadership Can Be Taught* by Sharon Daloz Parks (2005). Heifetz is also a physician who trained in surgery and psychiatry before devoting himself to the study of leadership in public affairs and business. As a cellist, he studied with Russian virtuoso, Gregor Piatigorsky.

Jews have faced adaptive pressures since Abraham.[1] We have survived by selecting the cultural DNA that is precious and essential over that which is not. We have conserved our core values, orientation, wisdom, and faith while internalizing the capacity to innovate—to take the best of our history into the future.

This work has thrived on the cultural predilection for healthy argumentation and discussion, an adaptive trait that Jews have nurtured over time in academies, schools, congregations, and even families. These institutions have become virtual pressure cookers that stir together different points of view and keep them in motion. They have inculcated a process that applies old wisdom to new challenges, encouraging successive generations to innovate new ways forward.

I find in my work that we have know-how for other cultures and peoples—especially those with their own post-colonial and diaspora experience—on ways to thrive in a changing and challenging world without losing their own best wisdom and tradition.[2]

Jewish History: Adaptability over Time and Circumstance

These lessons were drawn first in the Torah, Judaism's central narrative, which is read publicly, beginning to end, every single year, and which virtually underwrites the way "adaptive thinking" clarifies our highest values and tackles our toughest problems. It captures a time when changing technologies, population trends, and the emergence of empire politics strained the existing social and economic capacity of tribal societies and required new wisdom to prevent extinction.

First and foremost was the first agricultural revolution of twelve thousand years ago, which enabled people to settle down into village, city, and national life. For nearly two million years, humans had lived as foraging nomads in communities of less than forty people. Coordinating social and economic life, not for forty people, but for thousands, required new forms of governance, cultural norms, and social architecture. The Torah depicts the latter years of this enormous transition, thirty-five hundred years ago, as nomadic herdsmen (Abraham, Isaac, and Jacob) encounter Egypt, already an empire, and as Moses and the Israelites later struggle to sift through the culture and governance learned in Egypt to build something new and adaptive for all time.

Empires made sense. There is a compelling logic to habitual deference and authoritative command as effective means of governing large organizational systems and populations. But empires lack the adaptability to thrive in changing and challenging conditions. They become brittle. In the interests of uniformity and order they suppress the distributed intelligence that enables widespread innovation, moral development, and local adaptations to local environments.

The Torah introduces Judaism's discovery of "adaptive thinking." For thousands of years thereafter, such cyclical challenges as destruction, diaspora, and renewal refined it. For example, the response to Alexander the Great's importation of Greek culture (ca. 311 BCE), the ensuing Hasmonean revolt in 167 BCE (the one that gave us Hanukkah), and the Roman destruction of the Temple in 70 CE gave us the "Rabbis," the leadership group that developed "the oral law," the radical idea that learning is holy, and the insistence on submitting sacred texts to adaptive interpretation across generations. An ongoing diaspora was facilitated by collecting the foundational texts into a portable Bible. A centralized Temple and priesthood was replaced by a focus on family and the meritocracy of Rabbinic learning.

Technical Problems or Adaptive Challenges?

With this in mind, consider what my colleagues and I have learned as we have advised presidents and prime ministers, CEOs of business and not-for-profits, senior military officers, religious authorities, senior executives in public institutions, and people practicing leadership in the middle of things—in social movements, schools, congregations, community organizations, neighborhoods, and families.

We find that the most common source of leadership failure is diagnostic: people treat adaptive challenges as if they were technical problems. Problems are *technical* when the systems and processes of an organization or society work well. The answers to such problems are largely known already by some manager, authority, or expert—somewhere. Problem-solving is largely a matter of finding the right people. By contrast, *adaptive challenges* are less amenable to authoritative expertise and command. Their solutions are not already known; they require discovery and social learning as people face the collective need to change their attitudes, values, and behavior to develop new capacities.

Dispensing expert solutions to technical problems is a very different process of problem-solving than changing people's minds, hearts, and behaviors to achieve adaptive change. Adaptive challenges demand leadership beyond managerial or authoritative expertise. They demand practices that generate innovative experimentation, social learning, and, often, difficult transitional change. Adaptive change can be threatening because it requires mobilizing a community to accept partial losses as it sifts through its cultural DNA to determine what to conserve and what to discard, and then to develop new DNA, to survive and thrive.

Unfortunately, in times of uncertainty and distress, people yearn for easy answers—technical solutions—that minimize the discomfort of ambiguity and the pains of change. We invest our authorities with more answers than they have, creating markets for charlatans and demagogues. "Instead of looking for saviors, we should be calling for leadership that will challenge us to face the problems for which there are no simple, painless solutions."[3]

The Torah's Models of Adaptability

The Torah does that through a model of leadership that promotes the adaptive work of reconceiving civic life and modes of governance. It insists that *those invested with authority, human or divine, must practice the self-discipline of building collective capacity, rather than succumb to the temptation of generating perpetual dependency*. The Torah records our cultural evolution from dependency to widely distributed leadership, demonstrating how a people, enslaved for generations, became a society outfitting its members for collective responsibility.

Biblical Israel managed to anchor civic norms of authority not in the absolute power of kings but in the shared authority of prophets and priests as well, all answerable to the same divine authority. Distributing civic power among three institutions created norms of accountability anchored in the sanctity of civic trust. Moreover, instead of attaching leadership just to those in authority, all Israel was to be a "kingdom of priests and a holy people" (Exodus 19:6). Ordinary "followers" were to become engaged citizens providing leadership and mobilizing adaptability wherever needed.

Then, in Rabbinic times, *we learned how to learn*. As Rabbinic tradition puts it, we became God's partners in the ongoing work of creation. *From Bible to Rabbis, we learned that leadership generates capacity, not dependency.*

In short, our ancestors taught us how to move

- from absolute to shared authority,
- from responsibility lodged in authority to responsibility shared by a community, and
- from the uniformity of empire to the holiness of learning.

▲ ▽▲▽ ▲▽▲ ▽▲▽ ▲▽▲ ▽ ▲

The Heart of Darkness

Dr. Barbara Kellerman

Dr. Barbara Kellerman is the James MacGregor Burns Lecturer in Leadership at Harvard's John F. Kennedy School of Government. Among the sixteen books on leadership and followership that she has authored, co-authored, edited, and co-edited are: *Bad Leadership: What It Is, How It Happens, Why It Matters* (2004); *Followership: How Followers Are Creating Change and Changing Leaders* (2008); *Leadership: Essential Selections* (2010); *The End of Leadership* (2012); and, most recently, *Hard Times: Leadership in America* (2014). In 2015 and 2016 she was ranked by Global Gurus as #13 on the list of "World's Top 30 Management Professionals." In 2016 she received the Leadership Legacy Lifetime Achievement Award from the International Leadership Association.

My father was born in Vienna, Austria, in 1897, and my mother in Dusseldorf, Germany, in 1913. They each moved to Paris in the early 1930s, where they met and were married in 1936. Their honeymoon in Nice was dedicated in part to procuring visas to the United States. In February 1937, they set sail for New York.

Other members of my parents' families—all, like my parents, Jews—were less fortunate or prescient, depending on how you look at it. Most managed to escape in various harrowing ways. One did not: my father's brother fled Vienna for Prague after the *Anschluss*. But subsequent to 1942 he was never heard from again.

I reference this not as atypical self-disclosure, but as typical self-reflection: self-reflection on how I got to where I am, a longtime student/scholar of leadership based for the last fifteen years at the Center for Public Leadership, an enduring gift from Leslie and Abigail Wexner to the Harvard Kennedy School. That my professional life has been dedicated to the study of leadership is, it seems to me, a direct consequence of the family history encapsulated above. In my household, leadership was not just a subject of great intellectual interest—"Churchill," I was always told, was my first word—but a matter of life and death.

This more than anything else explains why I became a charter member of the "leadership industry"—my catchall term for what has become in the last thirty or forty years a burgeoning multi-million-dollar-a-year business, with countless leadership centers, institutes, programs, courses, seminars, workshops, experiences, books, blogs, articles, websites, webinars, videos, conferences, trainers, consultants, and coaches, most of which, of whom, claim to teach how to lead. My point here is not to question the claim, but to remark on how the field has evolved in recent decades, which has been to focus far more on leadership development and far less on leadership research.

Leadership has always been a subject of study and pedagogy—think Confucius, Plato, Machiavelli, and John Locke. But now it is an industry, a national and even international obsession, or fashion if you will, a vessel into which we pour enormous amounts of time and money on the assumption that people, lots of people, can learn how to lead wisely and well. But, as we have come to fixate on developing *good* leaders, we have taken to avoiding *bad* leaders. Bad leadership, however defined, has been relegated to the margins of our professional consciousness, in part at least because the field has strongly skewed toward teaching *how* to lead, and away from teaching *about* leadership.

The reasons for this have everything to do with where the money is, and nothing to do with how the world works. For as anyone not living in the proverbial cave can testify, the world is thick with bad leaders. Which is precisely why bad leadership should be as much a cause of our collective consternation as good leadership is a cause of our collective aspiration.

Until the advent of the leadership industry, the word "leader" was usually value free. It had no moral implication. A leader was no more and no less than someone who led, by whatever means necessary, toward whatever the designated end. Hannah Arendt, for example, used the words "leader" and "dictator" interchangeably. In her classic tome *Origins of Totalitarianism,* she wrote, "In the center of the movement, as the motor that swings it into motion, sits the Leader. He is separated from the elite formation by an inner circle of the initiated who spread around him an aura of impenetrable mystery."[1] It was James MacGregor Burns who, in his seminal book *Leadership*—something of a bible in the leadership industry— muddied the semantic waters. He distinguished between "leaders," who were good, and so-called "power wielders," who were bad. "Leaders," he argued, arouse, engage, and satisfy the motives of others, of their followers. "Power wielders," in contrast, are motivated by themselves, by their own needs, wants, and wishes. "Power wielders may treat people as things," Burns wrote. "Leaders may not."[2]

About a quarter century into the leadership industry it became clear that good leadership was becoming the center of our collective attention. It became similarly clear that bad leadership was being, to understate it, sidelined. We scarcely look at bad leadership, which is precisely why, now as then, in 2016 as in 1936, we have hardly any idea of how to stop or even slow it.

This has not in the past nor does it in the present sit well with me. In response to this drift, this shift to the sunny side, in 2000 I wrote an essay entitled "Hitler's Ghost: A Manifesto." It was my so far still largely futile attempt to turn the tide, to get the leadership industry to be more inclusive and integrative. This was my conclusion—and my prediction:

> Hitler's ghost cannot be, nor should it be, cleansed from our collective consciousness. If we insist on continuing largely to ignore what Bishop Tutu calls, "the depth of depravity," or for that matter the far paler shadows thereof (for example, thoughtlessness, stupidity, and

incompetence), Leadership Studies will atrophy. In fact, as the opportunities for further explorations increase, particularly from the social sciences to the hard sciences, to turn away from the full range of human behavior is to be, quite simply, irrelevant.[3]

My use of the term "Leadership Studies" was deliberate. For in keeping with what the academy most values, as well as with Jewish tradition, what we need in the field of leadership is more scholarship. So long as we remain fixated on leadership *development*, the field will be intellectually constricted and practically constrained. Moreover, by excluding bad leadership and—as important—bad followership from our collective consideration, we avoid expanding and enriching our understanding of what happens in the real word. For it, invariably as inevitably, includes the bad and the ugly along with the good.

After the Second World War was over, some Jews vowed, "Never again." Other Jews thought, "No need"—no need for such an oath, for never again will Jews be forced to face an existential threat. Now we know better. Now we know that the worm can turn, that anti-Semitism can and does return and with a vengeance. What we also know is that Hitler's ghost still haunts—that now as before it can be and often is tyrants, tyrannical leaders, petty and otherwise, who dictate what happens, while their followers choose or are compelled to go along.

So how can we continue to ignore what is endemic to the human condition? How can we continue to turn a blind eye to leaders and followers who go rogue? How can we continue to view the world through rose-colored glasses—when the heart of darkness is everywhere, every day in evidence?

I maintain that we have a moral obligation to pragmatism—to see the world as it is, not as we would wish it to be. I maintain that to honor Leslie Wexner in the present and, more importantly, into the future is to do no less.

▲ ▲▼▲ ▲▼▲ ▲▼▲ ▲▼▲ ▲

I've Never Experienced Anything Like the Times We Are In

Marty Linsky

Marty Linsky has been on the faculty of Harvard's John F. Kennedy School of Government for over thirty years, co-founded Cambridge Leadership Associates, and taught in all three of The Wexner Foundation original programs. His most recent publication (with Maya Bernstein) is *Leading Change Through Adaptive Design*. He is currently working on a book tentatively titled *Living Adaptively: If Your Horse Is Dead, Dismount*. Lurching toward retirement and dotage, he is passionate about nurturing the karma of a great vacation in his everyday life; exercising daily to avoid back surgery; rooting for his beloved Red Sox; traveling with his wife (Lynn Staley), children, grandsons, and friends; and decluttering after seventy-five years of accumulating endless useless stuff.

We all think we live in interesting periods, but I've been hanging around for three-quarters of a century, and with the possible exception of a couple of years in those tumultuous 1960s, I've never seen anything like this.

Change—and rapid change, at that—is a constant. The future is uncertain and unpredictable.

For making good decisions, we have both too much and too little information. As a relatively new grandparent (twice in fifteen months), I have watched my sons and daughters-in-law dive into

Google and generate reams of (often contradictory) information on every issue of infant care that occurs to them in their imagination or arises in their reality. Sorting it all out becomes an all-consuming and often frustrating task. And yet, many big decisions that they have to make, about jobs, housing, savings, and purchases, are undertaken without the advantage of being able to reasonably assume what their lives and the world will be like a decade from now, or even a year from now.

I grew up in the 1950s, when change was slow and incremental. While the future can never be known for certain, it seemed back then to be more or less predictable. If you went to college, you were likely to get a job and to have only one or just a handful of employers during your professional life. Marriage, children, suburbs, grandchildren, and retirement were all in the cards, and most of the people I knew growing up played the hand they were dealt with utter predictability, save for a few personal twists and turns and a glitch here or there along the way.

Not so today. Think about it. Since the turn of the century, just a decade and a half, the world as we knew it has exploded, literally and figuratively: 9/11, the Arab Spring, climate change, the continuing technological revolution, globalization, disruptive business innovation, aging of the baby boomers and simultaneously the emergence of the millennials with very different values, the Great Recession, an expanding gap between the rich and poor, and stateless terrorism refashioning the nature of global conflict.

Not surprisingly, the Jewish world has mirrored the broader reality. Whether it is the decrease in affiliation, increase in intermarriage, struggles over inclusion, or the changing relationships between Israel and the Diaspora, no aspect of Jewish life, identity, or concern has been exempted from the turmoil.

Let's assume, which I do, that the new reality of constant, rapid change and uncertain, unpredictable futures is, if not the long-term "new normal," at least going to be with us for a while.

The question is, What kind of leadership is needed under these circumstances? How will you have to tweak your own leadership to thrive and make progress on what you care most deeply about?

I am convinced of the need for two critical elements of leadership to see us through these uncertain times: (1) the will to adapt to new realities; and (2) the courage to take responsibility for inventing the future.

Adaptation is difficult because it means letting go of practices, ways of being, behaviors, and even beliefs that have previously served you well. Of course, not all of them must be left behind, but choosing which ones to abandon can be agonizing. Out of necessity, Jews overall, both individually and collectively, have developed superb adaptation capacity, but not without leaving behind aspects of culture, practice, and values that have been important. But they are not immune to the pressures that inhibit the adaptability required today.

Taking responsibility for inventing the future is difficult, too, because it means acknowledging that the people in positions of authority do not have all the answers. They do not know with any certainty what the Promised Land looks like or how to take us there. Quite regularly, they have no better idea than we do. Even as I write this, see, for example, the appeal of Trump and Sanders in the U.S. presidential campaign.

So, how do you lead under these circumstances?

For starters, do not look to me or any other so-called scholars, experts, or authority figures for the answers.

Begin by looking in the mirror; then ask yourself two questions.

First, what have you done, or not done, that has contributed to the very reality you are trying to change? I'm sure you are doing lots of things that have helped make progress on whatever issues or challenges you care deeply about, but we are all co-creators of our current realities, so if you are part of your reality, then you are doing—or not doing—something that has helped to create the problems you are trying to address.

Second, what have you been unwilling to do that has prevented progress? What are your constraints and fears, and which of them must you address in order to move on?

After identifying and acknowledging your role, think next about retooling your leadership for conditions of constant change and future uncertainty. I offer six elements to go into your thinking.

1. **Adapt instead of just executing.** Focus on the hard choices of what values, practices, beliefs, and relationships have contributed to your success that you now must leave behind.

2. **Experiment instead of just searching for solutions.** Experiments are more appropriate when stepping into uncertainty: the stakes are lower, you can run more than one at a time, you can make midcourse corrections, and there is no failure because every experiment generates learning.

3. **Invent new practices instead of just searching for best practices.** When approaching the unknown, where no one has been before, your challenge is to invent the future, because the lessons of the past may no longer apply.

4. **Orchestrate conflict instead of just resolving it.** Conflict is the engine of change. Leadership now demands surfacing deep conflicts and nurturing those most directly involved as they work them through rather than ignoring them, on the one hand, or taking unilateral responsibility of resolving them, on the other.

5. **Practice interdependence instead of just relying on yourself.** In a global world with instant communication, you are not alone and cannot make progress alone. Look for unusual partners and alliances. Those who are most against what you are trying to do are also the most interested.

6. **Take care of yourself instead of just sacrificing your physical and emotional well-being for the cause.** Under difficult circumstances, it is tempting to work until you drop. Bad idea. The world, and whatever cause you care about, needs you to be at your A-game, and you cannot be at your best if you are not getting enough sleep, exercising, eating well, and receiving, in appropriate ways, the love and affection you need to feel like a whole person.

I'm not suggesting you stop doing everything you've been doing and start from scratch. Rather, I'm urging you to have the courage and the will to tweak your own leadership practices, your own behaviors—wherever you are operating from, whatever role you

play, however successful you have been, and whatever your title—
to address the current challenges as you understand them. As the
cliché (and the song by Dan Nichols) goes, "If you do what you've
always done, you'll get what you've always gotten."

The Leader as Negotiator

DR. BRIAN MANDELL

Dr. Brian Mandell teaches at Harvard's John F. Kennedy School of Government, where he is senior lecturer in public policy. He also directs the Kennedy School Negotiation Project at the school's Center for Public Leadership. His current work addresses the theory and practice of negotiation and conflict resolution, with an emphasis on multi-stakeholder consensus building in negotiations. An expert in experiential learning and in curriculum design and development, Dr. Mandell teaches graduate students, mid-career professionals, and top-level managers in business and government.

Great leaders are great negotiators. By letting others have it their way, they exercise their soft-power skills to mobilize people, utilize resources, and reimagine organizational processes for maximal stakeholder value. Leaders in the turbulent twenty-first century need to "see sooner faster," and one way of doing that is by negotiating with allies and adversaries—and beyond conventional organizational boundaries—in order to generate deal-driving coalitions across wide-ranging networks.

How do they manage that? What unique negotiation abilities characterize their work? How do they convert interpersonal and organizational barriers into value-creating opportunities? In short, how do these leaders use negotiation to navigate a world characterized by volatility, uncertainty, complexity, and ambiguity?

In a word, such leader-negotiators are uniquely able to reinforce their vision and communicate the need for decisive action; they do so using five key interlocking competencies. These leaders are (1) curious, (2) entrepreneurial, (3) collaborative, (4) risk-accepting, and (5) talent developers and institution builders. Let us briefly examine each of these in turn.

1. **Curious:** The leader as curious, investigative inquirer continuously challenges the status quo—standing still is seen as going backward and losing ground. Curiosity extends to organizational and business practices not just within but also beyond the organization's traditional domains—to see how others are doing. This involves asking the right questions at all managerial levels and then listening carefully so as to uncover potential sources of vulnerability and blind spots, as well as opportunities likely to generate new sources of value.

2. **Entrepreneurial:** The leader as designer, improviser, and strategist never accepts the "game" as given. Attention is relentlessly focused on the changing landscape of user-consumer benefit. Equally important is encouraging (and even outright soliciting) continuous feedback so as to learn, adapt, and influence the future. As a strategist, this kind of leader anticipates sources of resistance, scans the environment for business and community development opportunities, empathizes with the constraints and choices faced by counterparts, and incorporates all of this "real-time" knowledge into the next set of shaping moves.

3. **Collaborative:** The leader as convener, coalition builder, and collaborative problem-solver assembles the right people, at the right time, in the right sequence to address the right set of issues and subsequently builds the right "team of teams" to strengthen buy-in and produce sustainable results in a timely manner. The leader-negotiator fully understands the competitive nature of the "business" environment but understands also that collaborative problem-solving

grounded in knowledge-sharing platforms is essential for recruiting key stakeholders, promoting open innovation, and aggregating the best ideas to ensure organizational relevance and resilience.

4. **Risk-accepting:** The leader as master deal-crafter is a smart risk-taker who quickly gets beyond parties' superficial positions to comprehend the full and deeper set of underlying interests out of which deals may arise. Always focused on the prize, this deal-maker builds winning, cross-boundary coalitions composed of players with both contending and complementary perspectives for the task of collective problem-solving. At the same time, leader-negotiators are not naive: they recognize spoilers, who are, by definition, motivated to block or significantly delay a deal's implementation. The savvy leader-negotiator demonstrates sufficient flexibility to accommodate legitimate concerns but sufficient conviction also to contain and manage spoilers. Beyond addressing the *substance* of the deal, the leader uses interpersonal relationships (both at and away from the table) to massage the *process* of getting the deal done. By addressing issues and people, the leader-negotiator identifies hidden sources of value, maintains a high degree of relevance, and develops a keener sense of what needs to be conceded now in exchange for greater gains later. Such leaders consistently deliver on the triple bottom line—greater profitability, enhanced social value, and environmental sustainability.

5. **Talent developers and institution builders:** Leader-negotiators understand the need to attract next-generation talent. But attracting the best and the brightest does not happen automatically. Nor does it happen by nurturing smart and energetic people within one's own organization alone. Potential new recruits must be persuaded to renegotiate their prior loyalties and aspirations—both personal and professional. Such persuasion involves framing a compelling vision of future opportunities, followed by the intentional effort to distribute the work of leadership once these

new recruits do come on board. A further requirement is the necessary empathetic and active listening that is needed to overcome fears of change. At stake is the critical and larger task of negotiating a legacy with peers, colleagues, and community.

This brief catalog of characteristics begs the question of whether such leader-negotiators actually exist. They do. One such leader, whose work I have been privileged to observe firsthand over the past twenty years, is Les Wexner. He is truly that curious observer who acts decisively. He is a brilliant strategist. He builds collaborative high-performing teams. He crafts complex value-creating deals. And he attracts first-rate talent to ensure innovation in, and long-term success of, top organizations in the business and philanthropic spheres. But more than this, Les has used his creative negotiation skills to foster the kind of community- and institution-building that encourages people to care about issues and challenges well beyond their own personal concerns. Les is an exemplar of the leader as negotiator.

Leaders and Managers

Divergence and Convergence

Larry Moses

Larry Moses has been with The Wexner Foundation for three decades. After thirteen years as its president, he is now the foundation's senior philanthropic advisor. He was the founding director of the Wexner Graduate Fellowship Program in 1987. As Leslie and Abigail Wexner's senior advisor, he plays a key role in organizing the family's philanthropic activities. He sits on numerous international, national, and regional boards, both civic and Jewish, including the Jewish Funders Network, Hillel International, and the External Advisory Committee of the USC Shoah Foundation's Visual History Archive. His articles and presentations, often centering on the challenges of leadership in modern Jewish life, have been widely circulated. He and his wife, Dr. Susan Steinman, are the parents of Dr. Alana Moses and Danielle Moses.

During the final years of Florence Melton's life, I visited her apartment every month to mine her formidable wisdom and to simply bask in her presence. We drank tea, and she reflected on Jewish life, bringing to bear over ninety years of experience and engagement. On one particularly memorable morning she stared hard into my eyes and said, "The problem with Jewish organizations is that we tend to be over-managed and under-led; we tend to be formulaic." It was not the first time I encountered some version of this insight, but Florence's intensity brought the idea to life for me in a Jewish context as never before. I have pondered it for a long time.

How ironic that the Jewish community, so widely admired by other ethnic and religious communities, so advanced in its social service networks, and so institutionally accomplished in so many ways, might be "under-led." For decades, in Jewish communal life we have been calling practically everyone "leaders" and everything we do "leadership." We call volunteers "leaders," donors "leaders," and professionals "leaders." We call our most generous contributions "lead gifts." We have "leadership retreats" and "leadership missions" and "young leadership" divisions ... one can go on and on.

We have used and overused the words "leader" and "leadership" to a point where they lose all meaning.

Our myriad organizations and congregations are, in the main, well run, fiscally accountable, and reasonably productive. But are they well led, or are they "formulaic," as Florence contended—so steeped, that is, in past assumptions and practices that they are out of step with the ever-emerging changes and opportunities of today? Calling everyone a leader does not in and of itself make us well led.

To begin with, we confuse "leadership" with "management," a mistake extensively elaborated in the professional literature. Management is fundamentally about the use of authority in organizational settings. In John Kotter's words, it is about "coping with complexity." It is through good management that otherwise unwieldy organizations operate reliably, predictably, and efficiently. Management is a set of well-known processes (planning, budgeting, staffing, assessing, controlling) that enable organizations to produce goods and services. Management brings order and consistency to the workplace. Without management, there is chaos. I do not denigrate the role of management when I elevate the importance of leadership. Both are essential.

Management, however, copes with complexity, while leadership copes with change or, better, orchestrates it. In the words of our beloved late teacher Warren Bennis:

> To survive in the 21st century we will need a new generation of leaders—leaders, not managers. The distinction is

an important one. Leaders conquer the context—the volatile, turbulent, ambiguous surroundings that sometimes seem to conspire against us and will surely suffocate us if we let them—while managers surrender to it. Managers are people who do things right, while leaders are people who do the right things.[1]

But managers do not only manage, and leaders do not only lead. They alternate between leading and managing depending on time and circumstance. We need to master the skills of leadership (envisioning and mobilizing change) and of management (maintaining stability and productivity). Navigating this seemingly contradictory dance means asserting authority to protect the integrity of what we are about, but also challenging authority by questioning the very assumptions behind what we are doing.

Management and leadership are not contradictory; they are complementary points on a continuum of practice. Leader-managers balance and mix the two by drawing upon distinctive skill sets for each.

Clearly, today's Jewish leaders need to be adept at envisioning and orchestrating change, but also at implementing and sustaining it. On the ground, the process invariably involves the same person. Today's managers cannot avoid the responsibility of leading; today's leaders cannot afford to be unskilled managers.

An organization's culture is a critical factor in the work of leadership and management. Organizations are more likely to embrace change if they display resiliency, enable dissenting views, and value experimentation to the point of encouraging risks at the cost of periodic failures.

At The Wexner Foundation, I learned early on to be wary of settling for success—an odd idea on the surface. Of course we strive for success. But we have to avoid the common trap of becoming so invested in success, so comfortable with it, that we close ourselves off to the ever-newer possibilities of doing something better. Continually challenging successful programs with hard and even disruptive questions has been central to our culture. It is in the encounter between protecting/growing what has been achieved (on one hand) and assessing what might be changed, discarded, or reimagined (on the other) that the manager/leader wrestles: faithful stewardship, but also the imperative to increase one's impact by innovation and change.

Finally, the art of management itself has changed over time. In the traditional paradigm, one *leads people* but *manages work*. But as Alan Murray points out:

> [In the new economy] where value comes increasingly from the knowledge of people, and where workers are no longer undifferentiated cogs in an industrial machine ... people look to their managers, not just to assign them a task, but to define for them a purpose.[2]

Toward this end, managers increasingly understand that the use of authority is less effective than the use of influence. Once again, management and leadership intertwine.

The management/leadership dance addresses the emotional struggle between being the authority and challenging authority. In the first, we protect what we have built; in the second, we let go and build anew. Management secures stability and predictability; leadership drives the challenge to do better and work differently.

The Jewish People is not an ever-dying people, as some half-jokingly quip. To the contrary, we are an ever-adapting people, continually navigating and balancing continuity and change. And it was Jewish leaders, at every step, who led our ancestors through attacks, schisms, and setbacks to newly constructed self-understandings and achievements. If anything, this leadership imperative is the Jewish people's genius.

The mantle of responsibility in contemporary Jewish life requires us to manage and to lead, to preserve and to change— above all, to know the difference and to choose the right role at the right time, thoughtfully, skillfully, and with an appreciation that the bridge between the two is not a bridge too far.

▲ ▲▼▲ ▲▼▲ ▲▼▲ ▲▼▲ ▲

Four Kiwis and the Jewish Future

RABBI AARON PANKEN, PhD

Rabbi Aaron Panken, PhD, an alumnus of the Wexner Graduate Fellowship, is president of the Hebrew Union College–Jewish Institute of Religion (HUC-JIR). After receiving a BES in electrical engineering at Johns Hopkins University and ordination at HUC-JIR, he earned a PhD at New York University in the development of Rabbinic law, and as an HUC-JIR faculty member, he teaches Rabbinic and Second Temple literature. His publications include many articles, in both scholarly and popular modes, and a book, *The Rhetoric of Innovation* (2005), an exploration of innovation in Rabbinic law. A commercial-rated multi-engine, seaplane, and glider pilot and sailor, he lives with his wife, Lisa Messinger, and their two children in the New York area.

> "A psalm of David: God, who may stay in Your tent, who may dwell on Your holy mountain?"
>
> —PSALM 15:1

Hundreds of miles from the nearest Jewish institution, far from the trappings of regular civilization, four extraordinary guides taught me what it means to lead. I was part of a group of fifty traversing the Milford Track—"the finest walk in the world," it is said—a tough 34.3-mile hike through mountain passes, over swing bridges, and past endless waterfalls in a remote corner of New Zealand. These guides—Akiko, Anna, Moon, and Simonee—have probably never considered the abstract term "leadership," but they epitomized the task of leadership in serious and palpable ways that inform how we can sustain the next generation of our people.

> "One who lives without blame, who does what is right, and
> acknowledges the truth."
>
> —Psalm 15:2

They were almost superhuman: in peak physical condition, they ate up the miles with a smile on their faces and tended to every possible human situation with boundless competence. The teen recovering from ACL surgery who could not carry her heavy pack and probably should not have come along altogether: *handled*. The boots that you thought were broken in but were causing rather expansive and colorful blisters: *managed*. The faster hikers who sped ahead and felt bogged down by those behind: *tackled*. The stragglers who arrived in camp at 6:00 p.m. every night after hiking since 7:30 a.m.: *aided*. All this they did while identifying every bird and plant, swimming laps in ice-cold glacial ponds, teaching the geology of the terrain, and providing tasty meals, enthralling stories, and useful advice.

1. They loved what they did.
2. They worked together.
3. They were highly knowledgeable and willing to teach others.
4. As a team, they excelled in it all.

Our guides were completely at home in their surroundings. They reveled in the natural beauty and the privilege of just being there. Their nightly briefings on the next day's challenges were couched in simple truths but accompanied by the serious business of convincing us we could make it through: Walk a little slower; leave earlier; use poles on this part of the trail; leave earlier still to see the massive waterfall just off the track; wash your clothes here, dry them here; get water from this stream, hot drinks at the next stop, breakfast by 6:30 a.m.

The beauty was this:

1. They told us the truth,
2. so we had enough information
3. to meet the challenges,
4. feel supported, and
5. achieve at the highest level we could.

"Whose tongue is not given to evil; who has never done harm to
his fellow, or borne reproach for his acts toward his neighbor."

—PSALM 15:3

Our guides were remarkably diverse and showed the ability to collaborate across experiences and cultures. Akiko, from Japan, had competed in the Olympics and tended to the Japanese families in our group who might feel uncomfortable amid the English-speaking majority. Anna, a fast-walking young Kiwi attorney who had left the law to hike and guide, possessed wit and wisdom that enlivened presentations and helped the evenings pass delightfully with humor. Moon, a Korean ski instructor was (astoundingly) on his *124th* traverse of this track. His goal: to break the standing record of 217 trips. Simonee, another young Kiwi, flitted up and down the trail—a social butterfly ensuring that everyone was thriving.

Their professionalism was extraordinary. When hikers got lost or did something less than optimal, they sorted out the situation quickly, gathered the flock, and kept us all moving in the right direction.

Through all five days,

1. they inspired confidence,
2. keeping us together,
3. without blame, reproach, judgment, or disparagement; instead:
4. simply working toward the goal in the best way for the entire group.

"For whom a contemptible one is abhorrent, but who honors
those who fear God; one who stands by an oath even to one's
own hurt."

—PSALM 15:4

On the hardest day of the hike, we walked 9.5 miles and crossed a vertiginous mountain pass that involved a vertical gain of 2,600 feet followed by a descent of nearly 3,000 feet. These figures may mean as little to you as they did to me before the hike—suffice it to say this was serious business. We covered dozens of switchbacks, walked through snow on the top of the pass, and watched fog cover the surrounding mountains. The only escape in the middle of the day was by medevac helicopter (a decidedly undesirable choice). From such lofty heights, the awe of God's creation was all-encompassing, and the sense of personal triumph sublime.

1. To stand by one's commitment, despite hardship and physical exhaustion, made for pride and inspiration at day's end.
2. Competent, confident, quiet, and self-effacing guides made a demanding and inspiring achievement possible.

"Who has never lent money at interest, or accepted a bribe against the innocent. One who acts in this way shall never be shaken."

—PSALM 15:5

Sir Edmund Hillary once said, "When you go to the mountains, you see them and you admire them. In a sense, they give you a challenge, and you try to express that challenge by climbing them." We admired the challenge God's mountains offered us, and we admired those who led us in conquering such challenges. To paraphrase the old Hasidic tale about Reb Zusya, we needed not to be Sir Edmund Hillary, but simply the best of who we are ourselves. Leadership enables everyone to become their best selves.

Jewish life is filled with challenges that can seem like intimidating hikes through unknown territory. What we need are guides who lead in the ways I learned from these four talented Kiwis. "One who acts in this way shall never be shaken."

▲ ▲▼▲ ▲▼▲ ▲▼▲ ▲▼▲ ▲

Showing Up
The Power of Presence

RAE RINGEL

Rae Ringel, founding president of the Ringel Group, is a certified executive coach and leadership trainer. She teaches at the Georgetown University Institute for Transformational Leadership and directs their Certificate of Facilitation Program. She specializes in enabling executives of corporations, nonprofits, and government agencies to become more effective managers and stronger communicators through developing a formidable leadership presence. Rae also offers deep experience in the areas of fund-raising and board development. She is an alumna of the Wexner Graduate Fellowship and is a faculty member for The Wexner Foundation. Rae lives in Washington, DC, with her husband and four children.

Zoom in. Daniel is a synagogue board president just moments away from soliciting the lead gift for a capital campaign to build a new sanctuary. This donor has financial capacity and enough communal standing to create momentum for others to join the campaign. Daniel feels the pressure, but he's prepared. He's done his homework, having researched the donor's giving history and past positions on all issues that might come up in the conversation. He has given himself plenty of time to get to the donor's house with a few minutes to spare.

As he is shown into the donor's sitting room, he reminds himself to be confident, gracious, and appropriately humble. He speaks in a low voice, and his comportment reveals the slightest hunch of his shoulders. He thanks the donor for his previous gifts and synagogue involvement. Then he launches into his request: "We both know why I'm here. I'm hoping you will contribute the lead gift for our campaign. It would set us up financially and set a standard for the rest of our community."

Zoom out. How's Daniel doing? Everything seems to be going okay. He's found a way to introduce the project and worked up the courage to make a clear request. But when we strip away the pleasantries, we find nothing left but a financial transaction. He is so consumed with closing the gift that he's failed to impart his vision, values, and passion. He hasn't listened to the donor, nor has he constructed a meaningful conversation in which to open up a space for something new to take hold.

For starters, Daniel lacks presence.

Leadership presupposes presence: among other things, the way we present ourselves, the physical stance we take, and the manner in which we approach the conversation. It is who we want to *be*, the "self" that we bring to the table when we show up.

Presence begins with getting centered. Between the car and the office, boardroom, or meeting room, clear your mind, slow it down, and think about how you are about to present yourself. How will you comport yourself? What energy will your voice convey? Who are you, and why are you there?

Language flows from presence, so having the right presence transforms the conversation that results. What if Daniel had seen his mission as truly sacred? He might have turned his request into an offer. What great questions might he have asked the donor to elicit his desire to be part of a great venture? What stories might he have had ready at hand to engage and inspire?

Zoom back in, as Daniel gets a second opportunity to make his ask—this time, with presence. He takes a few minutes to get centered, saying a prayer perhaps or reminding himself that the fate of the Jewish community depends on him today. He recalls his favorite Jewish text from *Parashat T'rumah*, a description of the first capital campaign in Jewish history: "Let them make me a sanctuary, that I may dwell among them" (Exodus 25:8). The Jewish People give in abundance at the prospect of experiencing the presence of God. "The divine of God in our synagogue," he thinks to himself. "Nothing less is at stake."

Surely God's presence is a matter warranting an offer, not just a request. What a difference the donor can make! With that thought in mind, Daniel enters the donor's house with presence—and with words that flow from it. His spine straight, his shoulders back, he says, confidently, "I'm so glad to have this conversation with you. We are engaged in a campaign upon which the community's Jewish future depends, and I get to be in a position to extend this invitation to you. I sit here with an offer, an offer to transform our community. I know you have some thoughts on the subject, so I want to hear from you about *your* vision. What does our synagogue community look like to you, up until now? What could it look like, moving forward? What role would you like to play in this vision? When you think down the road, what do you want your legacy to be?"

By now, the donor is engaged and leaning forward in anticipation. Presence is contagious. Now the donor feels his own presence being galvanized. The energy is palpable.

"Presence" can feel like a lightweight word, but it denotes something profound: the ability to connect authentically to the feelings of others through the sense of self that we bring to the table. It is a leader's very presence that is so impactful. Given the right presence, moreover, the right language follows. So too does the ability to engage the other person in an atmosphere that leaves a space for something new to emerge—a shared understanding of the partnership that leader and (in this case) donor share together. It transforms the way the donor feels about the entire organization. Presence invites presence. It invites donors in.

With proper presence, we are far more influential than we know. Presence derives from owning the importance of our message, embodying our values, and inviting others into the excitement of what we represent. Presence is the foundation for evoking trust and connection; it is the ground upon which exemplary leadership is built.

▲ ▲▽▲ ▲▽▲ ▲▽▲ ▲▽▲ ▲▽▲ ▲

Riding the Mood Elevator

DR. LARRY SENN

Dr. Larry Senn is chairman of Senn Delaney, an organizational culture-shaping firm that is part of Heidrick and Struggles. He has worked with dozens of Fortune 100 CEO teams, governors of states, members of two U.S. presidents' cabinets, presidents of major universities, and religious group leaders. The firm has reached over a million employees of Global 1000 firms around the world with concepts like the Mood Elevator. Dr. Senn is author of a number of books, including *21st Century Leadership*, *Winning Teams—Winning Cultures*, and *Up the Mood Elevator*. His latest book, *Riding the Mood Elevator*, is forthcoming.

Being Our Best Selves

There are times when we are at our best, the top of our game. These are the moments, hours, or days when we feel grateful, secure, confident, creative, and resourceful. We are more lighthearted, not as easily bothered by people and situations, less apt to "sweat the small stuff." We are more creative and resourceful and have better relationships—in part because we are more curious than judgmental, truly interested in people and ideas.

At times like these, we experience ease and grace. We move easily with life's flow and feel connected to wisdom, universal intelligence, or God. At times like these, we are traveling *"up* the mood elevator."

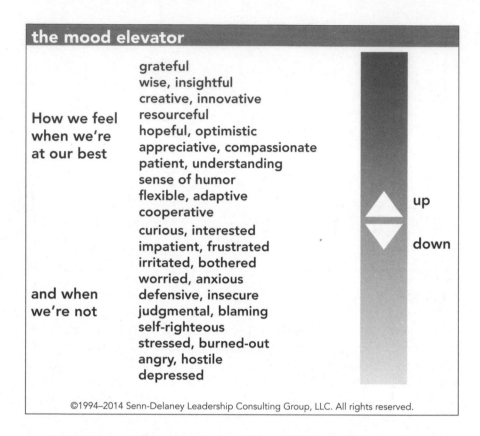

But being human means spending time "*down* the mood elevator" as well: times when life doesn't look or feel as good, when security gives way to worry, when we are easily irritated, more judgmental, on the defensive. We might also feel just generally down, inexplicably troubled—either passively (low energy, worry, or depression) or actively (feeling self-righteous or angry). The levels of the mood are just feelings we have, from grateful (at the top) to depressed (at the bottom).

The key to better relationships, less stress, and a richer, more successful and purposeful life is to spend more time on the higher floors of the mood elevator and to do less damage to ourselves and to others when visiting the lower ones. That's important, because we all visit the lower levels at times. Being human means having both highs and lows. The metaphor of an elevator catches our attention because it is so perfectly descriptive of our moods.

Although people relate immediately to the concept, very few think about their life experience in this way. They assume that nothing can be done about life's ups and downs—it's "just the way life is."

Indeed, we all spend some time riding up and down the elevator, visiting most of the floors at one time or another. But have you known anyone who willingly moved in at Impatient, Worried, or Judgmental? Those are places we may periodically visit, but certainly not where we'd like to take up permanent residence. Our stay on those lower floors can be much briefer and its impact significantly lessened, however, if we realize we are not totally at the elevator's mercy. Here are some elevator tricks of the trade.

Don't Blame Other People or Events for Your Moods

Most people explain their moods by external circumstances. If you ask them why they feel low, they will tell you about some event they didn't like or some person who pushed their wrong buttons. Maybe the stock market dived (again) or a boss or colleague blamed them for something they didn't do. Maybe they just stepped on the scale and didn't like the number they saw.

We encounter those challenges daily, if not hourly, but they don't explain where our moods come from.

Let me tell you a story about a friend named John, and let's see if you can figure out where John's moods originate.

John leaves work, having heard a rumor that the company is going to downsize and his area may be impacted. This upsets him so he stops at a park before going home and sits on a bench to try and regain his composure. What if he can't find another job? Will he lose his home? How can he cover college tuition for his son? With each new worry, he plummets further down the mood elevator from anxious, to worried, to downright depressed.

"Downsizing is a heartless thing to do," he thinks—a thought that induces judgment, then resentment and anger.

But wait, John recalls. Rumors like this have surfaced before and proved untrue. He moves back up the mood elevator to neutral and feeling a bit curious.

From this higher vantage point, a further thought moves him up to inspired and optimistic. "I hate this job. If this layoff really happens, I could take a severance package and start the business I've dreamed of."

Then he thinks of his family waiting at home and feels gratitude for the love they have for one another.

So what *did* cause John's wild fluctuations in moods? Right. It was his *thinking*! Each level on the mood elevator John visited was accompanied by a prior thought.

So It's Our Thinking That Creates Our Moods

Events may indeed trigger thoughts, but we are the ones doing the thinking. We create our own moods out of what happens to us. We see it in everyday life. We end a challenging day tired, overwhelmed by what we have to face tomorrow, and discouraged by what we didn't accomplish today. We get a good night's sleep, get up and take a walk, and miraculously, life looks fine. We start the new day more hopeful and optimistic. Nothing in our circumstances has changed. The only thing different is our thinking about it—the story in our head. Life happens to us all, but what determines our quality of life is what we make of it in our thinking. It helps to begin by noticing when your spirit drops or your intensity rises. Then, when possible, redirect your thinking. We call this a *pattern interrupt*.

The following two practices have the biggest long-term impact.

Take Better Care of Yourself

Have you ever noticed that when you are rested and more relaxed, you are more resilient? That it's harder for people to push your buttons? That you are not as easily irritated?

Our physical state impacts our mental resilience. Life usually looks better after a good night's sleep, a weekend off work, or a restful vacation.

Studies have shown that we catch colds more easily when we are run down; our physical immune system is weakened. So too with our moods. When we get run down and tired, it is easier for our thinking to go south. We are more sensitive to what other people say, take things more personally, and lack patience and understanding. As the quality of our thinking goes down, we become tired, even overwhelmed. We are not as wise or resourceful. As our effectiveness is hampered, we perceive more pressure and feel more stress.

With rest, however, our thinking becomes more reliable and less susceptible to creating those bad movies in our heads. Taking care of ourselves builds the resilience necessary to avoid plunging down the mood elevator. Adequate sleep and regular exercise head up the list of mood enhancers.

Count Your Blessings

It is no accident that gratitude is on the top story of the mood elevator. Gratitude is an overriding emotion. If you think about it, it is almost impossible to be grateful and angry or depressed at the same time. The calmness and warmth that accompany gratitude override sadness, impatience, irritation, and anger.

Also, because gratitude is an emotion that connects us to a higher spirit, we are more purposeful, present, and supportive of others when we are in that state of grace.

Since our thoughts create our feelings, spending more time thinking about all that we have to be grateful for is the mood elevator's express button to the very top floor.

To Do or to Be

Leadership Lessons from the Court of St. James's

Ambassador Daniel Taub

Ambassador Daniel Taub was recently appointed Director of Strategy and Planning for the Yad Hanadiv Foundation. Prior to this he spent 25 years as a diplomat and international lawyer, including as Israel's ambassador to the United Kingdom from 2011 until 2015. As an international lawyer in Israel's Ministry of Foreign Affairs, he specialized in the United Nations, counterterrorism and human rights law and was member of Israel's negotiating teams with Syria and the Palestinians. He writes and lectures widely on negotiation theory and international law. He holds degrees from the Universities of Oxford and London, and Harvard's Kennedy School of Government.

*T*o be or not to be ...

I hadn't given Hamlet's famous soliloquy too much thought until I became Israel's ambassador to the United Kingdom. No, I wasn't thinking of suicide. But I came to see the issue of leadership—and the idea of *being* a leader—in a new light.

For two decades and more I had thought of leadership in terms of *doing*. As a legal adviser in Israel's foreign ministry and a member of Israel's negotiating teams with its neighbors, I saw myself as effecting change primarily through advice and analysis, through backroom influence, through generating coalitions and seeding ideas.

A year as a Wexner Israel fellow at Harvard's Kennedy School of Government reinforced this approach. Leadership is less about the position you hold and more about the influence you have was a recurrent theme. That it can be exercised at every level was another—by going to the balcony, by building consensus, by thinking outside the box.

But landing at Heathrow Airport to take up my new post and being met by a crowd of security officers, embassy officials, and representatives of the British foreign ministry—and a convoy of diplomatic vehicles to match—was a sign that something was about to change.

Over the next few months I became used to a very different way of life. I was treated with a respect I had done nothing to deserve. I never had to open a door myself or even keep a house key in my pocket. I was in constant demand at events and functions—not because of anything I did but rather because of what I was, or more precisely, what I represented. Even distinguished communal leaders and hardened businessmen would open up emotionally and share sensitive confidences, as though my representing the Jewish state made me some kind of human Wailing Wall.

In this surreal new existence, leadership had little to do with what you *do*, but rather who you *are*.

But who was I? Within the embassy, even in my presence, people insisted on calling me "the Ambassador." Despite my pleas, the staff refused to call me by my first name, because they wanted the reminder that they were working with Israel's official representative. Similarly, when I would visit a Jewish school and be met with rows of children waving Israeli flags and singing *Hevenu Shalom Aleichem*, it took me a while to be able to put aside the bizarre notion that they were cheering me, personally, and to recognize that this was their way of showing love and care for Israel.

Even as I recognized that enabling people to connect tangibly with Israel was an important part of my function, the often passive nature of this role could be frustrating. I felt this most keenly during the Protective Edge military operation in Gaza. While two of our sons were in combat units on the front lines confronting missile and tunnel attacks, Zehava and I found ourselves in formal dress attending diplomatic and political events. I consoled myself by thinking that in some way we were re-creating the division of labor that created the State of Israel in the first place: members of the Yishuv defended their homesteads and cleared the marshes, while the Herzls and Weizmanns of the Zionist Movement made the case for the Jewish state in the salons of Europe.

But even if we were part of the same battle, it remained hard for me to credit this representative diplomatic function as being "real work." The real work, my instinct insisted, was what I did below the radar screen: building alliances and coalitions, channeling information, and developing strategies to advance Israeli interests in the United Kingdom.

Only slowly did I begin to realize that the public profile—the representative role—actually opened up possibilities. Being able to act in the name of Israel allowed me, for example, to express official appreciation to great British supporters of the Jewish state and the Jewish People. One such event, held in the British Parliament, was particularly moving: granting Yad Vashem recognition as "righteous among the nations" to a heroic group of British prisoners of war who had risked their lives to hide a Jewish girl from the Nazis inside their POW camp.

Having a diplomatic persona also allowed me to reach out to groups with whom Israel had had little or no connection. I enjoyed partnering with other ambassadors to host joint academic or cultural events, including, rather cheekily, a joint Hanukkah celebration with the Greek ambassador and a joint fast-breaking dinner with Moslem leaders when a Jewish fast day fell during the month of Ramadan.

A public profile was also invaluable in pushing back against campaigns of boycott and delegitimization. Articles and media appearances are important, but even more effective are personal visits—for example, to a university that has passed a motion to boycott Israel or to a city whose radical member of Parliament has declared it to be an "Israel-free zone."

In these and in other ways I came to appreciate that there are many models of leadership, including the public representative role, which should not be discounted.

Back in Israel, a regular citizen now, unaccompanied by security and needing again to remember to take my house key with me, I wonder what I can take from this experience.

It occurs to me that for many of us, alongside our functional positions there may also be a representative, even ambassadorial, dimension. Just being who we are, we represent the values of our ministry, our company, our charity, or our cause. And as we move up the ladder of our organization, we are increasingly looked at as a model of our organizational values.

It is tempting to dismiss this dimension and focus only on our practical action. But my experience suggests that what we are— our roles, positions, and titles—can be embraced and harnessed for what they allow us to do. They may allow us to put greater weight behind initiatives—not just ours but those of others. They may enable us to show appreciation to those who are undervalued. And they may empower us to resolve tensions and create synergies by using our standing to bring different groups together.

However we decide to use it, a formal position is not only an honor and a responsibility—it is also an opportunity. If we use it wisely, we may find that there are things we can achieve not only by doing, but also by being.

▲

Jewish Models of Leadership

Leading Change

A Lesson from Tamar and Judah

Maya Bernstein

Maya Bernstein is a co-founder and current associate at UpStart, an initiative to support innovation in the Jewish community. She facilitates workshops on change leadership, creativity, and innovation and is on the faculty for the Wexner Graduate and Heritage Foundations and for Georgetown University's Institute for Transformational Leadership. Her writing has appeared in the *Stanford Social Innovation Review*, the *Huffington Post*, and multiple Jewish publications. She and her husband, Noam Silverman, live in the New York City area with their children.

I remember the first course I took as a graduate student at Harvard's John F. Kennedy School of Government. On the first day of class, the professor opened by saying, "Let us begin," but then merely folded his hands and stood, a powerful, quiet presence, until the allotted time ended, when he added one more word, "Time," and left the room. The void he created led over half the students to trickle out—or to "check" out, even while staying in their seats.

A few participants tried to take the class into their own hands, including a retired army officer, who announced that we would be unable to learn about leadership unless we were in relationship with one another. He suggested that we should share something about our past and then spoke, for a full (seemingly endless) five minutes, after which he looked at me to go next. I did and then looked to a third person, who, however, objected, "There are over one hundred people in this room—it's a ridiculous idea." Silence reigned as I realized how, as per my default, I had automatically done what authority asked of me. I sat there, embarrassed, wondering: What if I were to think critically about the decisions being made around me? What if I chose what role to play, rather than take the one assigned to me?

That opening day at Harvard made visceral for me some differences between *leadership* and *authority*. Leadership is open to anyone; authority is the position granted to and held by someone in particular. Authorities are generally charged with protecting the status quo. Those who exert leadership disrupt the status quo, for the sake of change and growth. Those in positions of authority are easily tempted to avoid exercising leadership, which entails threatening the very order and stability that they are responsible for upholding.

Authority tells you what to do; leadership enables others to grow and change and exert leadership themselves. That said, authority figures can exert leadership as well. My professor, with plenty of authority, had the courage to subvert his traditional role in order to create an environment where insights about leadership might flourish. In the process, though, he disappointed many in the group and challenged traditional expectations of the graduate learning environment.

The biblical story of Judah and Tamar (Genesis 38) has a lot to say on the subject.

The story comes after several stories marked by a pattern of relationships marked by "who's in" and "who's out." Losers— those who do not fit in or who threaten the system—are killed off or expelled. With Cain and Abel, for example, one brother survives; the other is killed. Similarly, albeit less violently, with Abraham and Lot: Abraham stays where he is; Lot is sent away. We then get the familiar pattern of fathers choosing certain children and expelling others: Isaac over Ishmael, Jacob over Esau. The Judah/Tamar story comes on the heels of Joseph being thrown into the pit by his brothers. (The only twist here is that it is not his father who rejects him, but his brothers, who rebel against their father's choice of a preferred son.)

The background to the Judah/Tamar story is the biblical law of levirate marriage, which stipulates that if a man dies without an heir, his brother is obliged to marry and provide offspring through his deceased brother's wife. Judah's oldest son marries Tamar and dies, leading Judah to wed Tamar to his second son. When that son dies too, Judah fears for the life of his third son and so refuses to provide him next. It is as if he now casts Tamar away as unwanted—the old pattern of "who's in" and "who's out." If the pattern were to hold, Tamar would be "out" and not heard from again.

But Tamar breaks the pattern of acceptance or rejection. As a woman in a patriarchal society and a rejected wife at that, she has absolutely no authority, but she does exert leadership.

What exactly does she do? Unable to have children via Jacob's third child, she disguises herself as a harlot, sleeps with Judah himself to become pregnant, and then allows her pregnancy to be discovered. As she is about to be executed for her "crime" (the expected excluded role), she shows Judah his own staff and seal, which she took from him when they were sleeping together. Judah must now acknowledge that he is the father. Tamar risks her own life to reject the inevitability of being excluded. She knows that she has been wronged and exerts leadership to raise that issue for those who have authority and who have created the unfair circumstances.

Her doing so, moreover, permits Judah to rise to the occasion. "*Tzadkah mimeni*," he admits, "She is more righteous than I" (Genesis 38:26). Having changed the rules of the game, Tamar allows Judah to see her anew and take responsibility for the wrongdoing he was about to countenance.

What tremendous courage Judah shows in this acknowledgment. As patriarch, he has been the person with supreme authority, the man charged implicitly with maintaining the pattern of the past. He chooses instead to dare to think differently—to think for himself, to acknowledge Tamar's point of view, to subvert the pattern. In the future, his newfound perspective will create the space in which he is able to feel the pain of Joseph, his brother, and Jacob, his father, and ultimately to reconcile the family. When he recounts the story of his family to Joseph (Genesis 44:18–34), he does so with empathy. He acknowledges the wrong that he and his brothers did to Joseph, he shows his own vulnerability, and in turn, he empowers Joseph to break the pattern as well. Joseph welcomes his brothers back rather than branding them as "out" and having them killed.

Judah's line, in our tradition, is the messianic line. What if we were to think of leadership as the work of bringing about the messianic era? Would we do so by breaking patterns, refusing to abide by what is simply expected of us, taking risks (like Tamar), admitting error (like Judah), embracing reconciliation (like Joseph), and, by our creative example, challenging others to grow as well? Could we create a world in which empathy dictates our choices? A world in which everyone strives, continually, to grow, to learn, to lead? A system in which everyone "is in"?

▲▼▲▼▲▼▲▼▲▼▲▼▲▼▲▼▲

What Do You Stand For?

Dr. Erica Brown

Dr. Erica Brown is an associate professor at George Washington University and the director of the Mayberg Center for Education and Leadership. She is an educator and writer, whose ten books include *Inspired Jewish Leadership* (a Jewish National Book Award finalist) and *Take Your Soul to Work: 365 Meditations on Every Day Leadership*. She has served officially as scholar-in-residence for Jewish Federations in Greater Washington, D.C. and Boston. Dr. Brown was a Jerusalem fellow; is now a faculty member of The Wexner Foundation and an Avi Chai fellow; received the 2009 Covenant Award and the 2012 Bernie Reisman Award; has degrees from Yeshiva University, University of London, Harvard University, and Baltimore Hebrew University; writes a monthly column for the *New York Jewish Week*; and maintains a blog, Weekly Jewish Wisdom at ericabrown.com.

When you're a leader, you are often called upon to take a principled stand on issues. When you're a values-driven leader, the hope is that these values have been in formation for a long enough time that you don't have to waffle or stretch for an answer. You can stand tall as a person of integrity and authenticity. I think often of the words of Winston Churchill: "Courage is what it takes to stand up and speak."

"Courage is also what it takes to sit down and listen," Churchill added, and indeed, leaders do listen, but sometimes we stand even to listen, as when a judge asks defendants to rise to hear their sentence. Such standing is deeply symbolic of the fact that what's being said deserves honor and attention, and it goes back to a long-standing Jewish tradition, first mentioned in the closing chapter of Deuteronomy, when we gathered as a collective and stood to hear the words of the covenant.

> *You stand this day*, all of you, before *Adonai* your God—your tribal heads, your elders and your officials, all the men of Israel, your children, your wives, even the stranger within your camp, from woodchopper to water-drawer—to enter into the covenant of *Adonai* your God, which *Adonai* your God is concluding with you this day. (Deuteronomy 29:9–11)

In his JPS commentary on Deuteronomy, Professor Jeffrey Tigay observes that *nitzav*, the Hebrew term for "stand" here, is more formal than *omed*, the usual term in both ancient and modern Hebrew.[1] *Nitzav* denotes the way we presented ourselves before God to accept the divine covenant—not just "standing around" as it were, but standing in rapt attention to what matters. We find a similar usage in the book of Joshua: "Joshua assembled all the tribes of Israel at Shechem. He summoned Israel's elders and commanders, magistrates and officers, and they presented themselves [*vayityatzvu*, the reflexive form of the same Hebrew verb] before God" (Joshua 24:1). This act of "standing" for a covenant honors the ritual and offers ceremonial formality to the gathering. Our classic medieval exegetes explain that such standing has "a when," "a where," "a who," and "a why."

The famous eleventh-century French commentator Rashi explained "the *when*": it occurred on the very last day of Moses's life, when, no doubt, the followers who had never made his life easy would be more open and attuned to his message. Rabbi Abraham ibn Ezra, the twelfth-century Spanish commentator, explained "the *where*": everyone gathered around the Ark of the Covenant, the centerpiece, or heart, of the ancient Israelite camp.

Thirteenth-century French interpreter Rabbi Hezekiah ben Manoah explained "the *who*": from the most important to the very least, everyone was in attendance. Everyone needed to bear witness; everyone needed to sign off. For an experience of this magnitude, the very foundation of Jewish peoplehood, not one person could be absent.

Finally, we get to Nachmanides, the thirteenth-century Spanish commentator, who explained "the *why*": "You will stand and present yourselves before God to stand up for this covenant, to accept the Torah and its explanation." Standing was part of a collective oath, almost like a marriage ceremony that formalized a lifelong partnership with God. The message seems to be: "Stand here now so you will know what to stand up for in the future."

Samson Raphael Hirsch, a nineteenth-century German rabbi, correctly saw the act of standing as the symbolic posture of acceptance; he matched the verb with three adverbs: "standing firmly, energetically, and purposefully."

When presenting, teaching, or running meetings or programs, leaders make strategic decisions about when and when not to use what social psychologist Amy Cuddy calls a power pose. When should you stand, and when should you sit? The choice of position says a lot about the context and the speaker. The casual sense of sitting around a table in a boardroom creates one group feeling, whereas standing tall when advocating a position creates another.

Standing up for what you believe was important in biblical days and is no less important now. In leadership, we sometimes have to stand up to the opposition or take a stand. We may even have to stand up to friends who disagree—a much harder thing indeed. When we encounter wrongdoing, we say, "I won't stand for that." We designate people we respect as being "in good standing." They are people who "stand tall."

Rabbi Hirsch knew that how we stand may communicate even more than the content of what we say—standing up for something leaves the most lasting impression. There is an art to knowing how to choose a meaningful leadership posture. And when we stand, let us do so "firmly, energetically, and purposefully."

▲▼▲▼▲ ▲▼▲ ▲▼▲ ▲▼▲▼▲

Tears of Doubt

Rabbi Yochanan ben Zakkai's Spiritual Legacy

Dr. Ruth Calderon

Dr. Ruth Calderon is one of Israel's leading figures involved in reviving Hebrew culture and a pluralistic Israeli-Jewish identity. In 1989, she co-established ELUL in Jerusalem, the first *beit midrash* in which secular and religious women and men studied and taught together. In 1996, she founded ALMA, a Jewish liberal arts program for advanced learning. Dr. Calderon is the author of *A Bride for One Night*, a personal homiletic reading of Talmudic legends, and *Talmudic Alpha Beta*. From 2013 to 2015, she was a Knesset member from the Yesh Atid Party, where she was deputy speaker, member of the Education and State Control Committees, and chairperson of the Lobby for Jewish Renewal. She holds a master of arts and PhD in Talmud from the Hebrew University of Jerusalem.

Like a stonemason extricating a brick from a wall, I have pried loose a brick from the stories our sages tell about the formative days of Rabbinic Judaism. This Talmudic brick portrays a message of leadership that I now add to The Wexner Foundation, that magnificent edifice dedicated to leadership development, which I have been fortunate to benefit from in various ways.

It is the deathbed story of one of the greatest leaders Rabbinic Judaism has known. He was the man who fashioned the new world that burst into being after the destruction of the Second Temple. He founded the new rabbinic center of Yavneh. His name was Rabbi Yochanan ben Zakkai. In our own era, he might be compared only to David Ben-Gurion, a man who, by standing at the crossroads of history and making decisions, altered the face of Jewish destiny. Ben-Gurion constructed the modern State of Israel; Ben Zakkai created Rabbinic Judaism itself.

Rabbi Yochanan ben Zakkai witnessed the end of an earlier era: the War of 70 CE and the Roman siege of Jerusalem.

In the case of Jerusalem, he was struck especially by his people's behavior within that city under siege—the radicalism, the infighting, the zealots who burned the granaries and lumber storehouses to hasten the end, the zealot leadership that lost control of its people—and he reached the terrible conclusion that Jerusalem could not be saved. He took action to extricate himself from Jerusalem and attempted to find a modicum of comfort outside the city walls.

He made over that "modicum of comfort," however, into an altogether new Jewish world, a revolutionary one that could exist beyond the Temple precincts. From then on, Jewish community anywhere in the world would be the mainstay, not the Temple; prayers would replace animal sacrifices; leadership would pass from priests to rabbinic sages. All this Rabbi Yochanan ben Zakkai established in Yavneh, the city whose Hebrew name can literally be read as "[may] it be built."

Now comes the story I wish to tell.

Customarily, in Rabbinic culture, as described in the Babylonian Talmud, when a sage was terminally ill, the entire learning community would gather in his home to replicate the aura of a study house in all its glory. This would allow the sage to depart from them while retaining his stature as an authoritative Torah scholar, notwithstanding the frailty of his body. So, too, when it came time for Rabbi Yochanan to die, his disciples came to take his leave, asking of their dying master a spiritual will, a legacy, some final words of Torah that would summarize what his current status between life and death—beyond the bounds of personal honor, obligation, and societal norms—could allow him to share.

So far, we have just another deathbed story—Rabbi Yochanan ben Zakkai's disciples visiting him at home. But in this case something unprecedented happens: when he sees them, he begins to weep. The students have never seen their master cry, however; they have always relied on him to be a source of strength and confidence.

They say to him, "Lamp of Israel, pillar of the right hand, mighty hammer! Why are you crying?" That is to say, please stop crying and resume your role as omnipotent leader, the one who speaks and is obeyed, the architect of the new Jewish era.

But Rabbi Yochanan is not afraid to cry; in fact, the opposite is true.

It seems to me that this crying—this gesture beyond words that breaks down the barriers of convention—is the act by which Rabbi Yochanan shakes himself free of his official position and permits himself to share the doubt he has been carrying all these years. It is, in itself, his spiritual legacy.

He depicts this moment of imminent death as a trial and confesses, "I am about to be judged by the Holy One, blessed be God, and I do not know the path on which I will be taken, to the Garden of Eden or to *Gehinnom*."

The horrendous doubt that Rabbi Yochanan ben Zakkai has been shouldering is the uncertainty facing any true leader. In Rabbi Yochanan's case, it began that fateful day when he decided that the Jews of Jerusalem were irredeemable and he must escape the city. Having made that choice, he forged ahead with what had to be done: establishing Yavneh, formulating prayer services to take the place of the Temple sacrifices, developing Torah study, and anointing rabbinic scholars as the new leadership. But beneath it all, beneath the apparent certainty, the bravado, even, of leadership, he harbored within himself the doubt that is integral to leadership: Had it been necessary to leave? Had he done the right thing? Could Jerusalem have been saved?

Until the day of his death, Rabbi Yochanan has played the role of leader, hiding the nagging misgivings, lest his followers be distracted from focusing on the task at hand.

Now, on his deathbed, however, the master wishes to teach his disciples one final lesson: the need to integrate even their doubts into their leadership. Real problems are really complex; hard decisions are always open to question. While productive solutions must be boldly pursued, doubts are inevitable for leaders who possess ethical, values-oriented, historical depth, leaders who are multidimensional. And these doubts must be nurtured also, because every revolution no matter how just, every cultural enterprise no matter how beautiful, runs the risk of turning into a one-dimensional, superficial ideology over the course of time. Only by internalizing doubt alongside certainty can true sages avoid the abyss of overconfident certitude that leads to disaster.

Why exactly did Rabbi Yochanan weep? Was he simply overwhelmed by the magnitude of the occasion? Did he recognize in his students the perilous naiveté of the second generation after the revolution? The Talmudic narrator does not explain. So Rabbi Yochanan ben Zakkai's final song remains an autonomous work of art, like the deathbed haikus that Zen masters customarily wrote before their deaths—the one composed by Soa (1677–1742), for example: "Whether or not a paradise awaits in the far reaches of the west."

All we can do is tell the story, as I have here, allowing it to echo in the minds of those who read it, so as to help them contemplate the complexities of certainty and doubt and allow them too to weep on occasion, even as they see their historic task through to completion.

The Impossible Task of Jewish Leadership

Rabbi Edward Feinstein

Rabbi Edward Feinstein is senior rabbi of Valley Beth Shalom in Encino, California, and an instructor at the Ziegler Rabbinical School of the American Jewish University. His first two books, *Tough Questions Jews Ask: A Young Adult's Guide to Building a Jewish Life* and *Jews and Judaism in the 21st Century*, were National Jewish Book Award finalists. His *Capturing the Moon* retells the best of classic and modern Jewish folktales. His latest book, *The Chutzpah Imperative*, traces the Jewish celebration of human responsibility. Rabbi Feinstein shares life with his wife, Nina, and three college-age kids. Every Friday afternoon, he bakes brownies from a recipe revealed to his ancestors at Mount Sinai.

Is "Jewish leadership" an oxymoron? We are a people delivered out of tyranny. Having escaped the servitude of Egyptian despots, we live with an unyielding suspicion that every leader is tomorrow's Pharaoh.

Even Moses is subject to our skepticism. In his first encounter with Israelites, he slays an Egyptian taskmaster who is beating a Hebrew slave and then intervenes in a fight between two Hebrews, demanding of one of them, "Why do you strike your fellow?" This Hebrew retorts, "Who made you chief and ruler over us?" (Exodus 2:11–14).

Yet we know that without strong leaders, we abandon our identity and stray from our core principles. Moses remained on

Sinai just forty days when we ganged up on Aaron and demanded a god of gold (Exodus 32:1), and an entire book of the Bible, the book of Judges, is a polemic about life without leadership, a time of moral and political chaos. The book's last line laments, "In those days there was no king in Israel; everyone did as he pleased" (Judges 21:25).

We need strong leaders, but we have no faith in those who lead us. From the Bible on, this ambivalence becomes deeply etched into the Jewish collective identity.

The Bible offers a resolution, however: a trifold leadership of king, prophet, and priest.

The king has all executive power. He collects taxes and runs the state, adjudicates conflicts and keeps the peace, raises an army and defends the kingdom. Kings are pragmatic, balancing visions of the ideal with conditions of the real. They make compromises, choosing among competing goods or, more commonly, lesser evils. Their power is legitimated by the wisdom of its use and by its consequences.

In the biblical model, the king enjoys no symbols of the sacred: his crown and scepter are not religious emblems. There is no inherent sanctity to his kingship. His authority is purely functional— every use of his power must, therefore, be justified. Even King David, the greatest of Israel's kings, the progenitor of the Messiah, is brutally castigated by the prophet Nathan for killing his neighbor and stealing his wife. Being king does not put one above God's law. The king is accountable.

It is the prophet who carries this message. The prophet is the nation's conscience. He incessantly and adamantly demands moral purity. His power derives from his moral passion. He has no worldly power. His authority is vested in his role as voice of our values.

There is always tension between prophet and king. No government, no leadership can be morally pure. All leadership is ultimately a matter of negotiating compromises. Diplomacy, policy, planning, budgeting—any leadership decision is a matter of trading away some principles to preserve others. The king insists,

"This is the best we can do." The prophet responds, "It's not good enough!"

Were a prophet to find himself invested with worldly power, he would soon despair. No wonder Moses was not allowed into the Promised Land—into the real world of limitations and accommodations! Plato was wrong to propose the model of a philosopher-king. Philosophers, like prophets, deal in the realm of the pure, the theoretical, the ideal. They make very poor kings. Philosophers and prophets who find themselves in power become tyrants. They use their power to force the complexity of the world into the simplicity of their moral vision. And they murder those who oppose them. Think Robespierre, Lenin, Mao.

Kings need prophets. The tension between them is essential. Those in power need to be reminded of the ideal and the pure. They need to hear truths so that when they make moral compromises, they know what they're compromising. The necessary is not ideal; the pragmatic is not perfect.

The biblical model builds in tension and conflict. Prophets demand more of kings. Kings resent prophets' impracticality and dreamy idealism. How does the system hold together? Who keeps the king from killing the prophet, or the prophet from deposing the king? That's the job of the priest. The priest is responsible for the sacred precincts. His hands alone touch the consecrated objects, the holy symbols of God's presence. He bears our collective narrative, our shared memories—how we began, the ideals that motivated us, the heroism of our founders. The priest is inseparable from his uniform, the symbol of our collective endeavor, our community's dreams. It is the priest, therefore, who is charged with making peace, holding us together in solidarity, despite our tensions. He is the one who reminds us how far we've come, how deeply we've invested in one another, and how much more there is to do together.

King, prophet, priest. Every Jewish organization needs these roles. At every meeting and moment of decision, we easily gravitate to the pragmatism of the king, making hard decisions about the future. But someone needs to play prophet and insist that we reach for our dreams. Yes, there will be tension. That's built in. That's creative leadership. But someone needs to raise the emotional temperature of the room because too much is at stake to let this go by easily. (Hint: If you sit on a board that finishes important meetings early, without disagreement, without emotion ... you've killed off your prophets. Stand up and be the prophet.)

And someone needs to be our priest, to remind us of our narrative and ensure that we hold together. (Another hint: If you sit on a committee that argues and argues and gets nothing done, or a committee so tense that afterward people stand in the parking lot bickering endlessly, you've excluded your priest. Stand up and be that priest.)

Is this any way to lead a people? It is a model filled with conflict, tension, and stress. It isn't orderly or clean or decisive. But it befits a people who share the Torah's lofty vision for a world redeemed and repaired, but who know the realities of this world all too well. It befits a people so utterly idealistic and yet so deeply realistic. The Talmud captures this well. We are taught: If you are planting a tree and you hear that the Messiah has arrived, first finish planting the tree; then go see if it's true.

▲▼▲▼▲▼▲▼▲▼▲▼▲▼▲▼▲

First Plant the Sapling

Beyond Messianic Leadership

Rabbi Lisa J. Grushcow, DPhil

Rabbi Lisa J. Grushcow, DPhil, is a member of the Wexner Graduate Fellowship, class 12. Her ordination is from the Hebrew Union College–Jewish Institute of Religion, in New York (2003). She serves as senior rabbi of Temple Emanu-El-Beth Sholom, the only Reform congregation in Montreal. Prior to her rabbinic studies, she earned master's and doctoral degrees from Oxford University, where she studied as a Rhodes Scholar.

At the installation of my rabbi and teacher Rabbi Robert Levine as senior rabbi of Congregation Rodeph Sholom in Manhattan in 1991, the chair of the Search Committee, Jack Levitt, shared these words:

> [The] modern rabbi should now be a scholar, learned in Torah and the texts; an exemplar and transmitter of Jewish values; a teacher of adults and children.... He or she must prepare and deliver two sermons weekly, profound in their import, light in their touch, witty in their references, full of literary allusion, provocative but reassuring, inspiring and soothing. That rabbi should attend a number of funerals and officiate at several weddings each week, not to mention bar and bat mitzvahs.... That rabbi should be expected to meet with congregants, if possible

at their and not the rabbi's convenience, to commiserate, counsel, and help them with spiritual problems, health crises, family crises, practical worries. The rabbi should of course attend board meetings and committee meetings and staff meetings and school meetings and neighborhood clergy meetings.

It is essential too that the rabbi should be a voice for social justice, both in and outside the congregation, in the prophetic tradition of our people. And certainly we would expect no less of the rabbi than to concern him- or herself with the practical needs of the congregation, budgets and fund-raising.

To Jack's long list, I would add: finding the secret to sustainability in synagogue life and, of course, being the paradigm of a perfect parent and partner. The list is very long.

From Rabbi Levine I learned many things, but two stand out: First, presence matters. People need to know that you're there. Second, *tafasta m'ruba lo tafasta*—if you strive for too much, you will accomplish nothing. These two contrary pieces of wisdom accompany me wherever I go, along with the problem they entail: How to be everywhere, doing everything for everyone, while recognizing our own limitations? How to lead and serve, without shortchanging our families and those we love?

We can learn much about this dilemma from the foundation myth of Yochanan ben Zakkai, the rabbi said to have saved Judaism in the wake of the Roman destruction of Jerusalem. Legend has him escaping the siege by posing as a corpse and being carried out of the city in a coffin. For successfully predicting that the conquering general will be the next emperor, he is rewarded by the gift of Yavneh as a city to raise up rabbis.[1] From his actions, Rabbinic Judaism arises like the phoenix from the ashes.

In actuality, Rabbinic Judaism preexisted Yochanan ben Zakkai and then took centuries more to be established as normative Judaism. But Rabbi Yochanan is credited with it all. He is the quintessential messianic and visionary leader whom modern Jews would gladly hire as their senior rabbi. He is not altogether unlike another first-century Jew: Jesus, whose death and resurrection become Christianity's founding story. Such founding legends practically ensure the yearning for leaders to be messianic.

But messianic expectations carry serious drawbacks. A provocatively titled article by Tomas Chamorro-Premuzic wonders, "Why do so many incompetent men become leaders?" Because, he argues, we mistake confidence for competence. We need the latter, but hire for the former, mistaking "manifestations of hubris — often masked as charisma or charm ... for leadership potential."[2]

What enables these usually male managers to rise to the top of the corporate or political ladder may lead also to their downfall, because what it takes to get the job is the reverse of what it takes to do the job well.[3]

When it comes to hiring leaders, men, it turns out, who are more often seen as confident, win out over women, who may actually be more competent. Hence, the stained glass ceiling of the rabbinate, where women are hired for assistant/associate positions and passed over for senior rabbinic posts. Even beyond gender, organizations hire people who give the impression they can single-handedly save the day — people with messianic expectations of themselves, that is.

Upon entering my position as senior rabbi of Montreal's venerable Reform synagogue, Temple Emanu-El-Beth Sholom, my greatest single mistake was overconfidence in what I could accomplish and how quickly I could accomplish it. I would so love to be the hero who swoops in and solves the problems of Jewish life. But leadership is usually the less heroic task of making the best possible decisions, day by day, in consultation and not alone. I have learned to value small steps forward rather than awaiting messianic breakthroughs. As Leslie Wexner once said, "We should be doing rather than waiting for Godot or the Messiah."[4]

Here, Yochanan ben Zakkai has something to teach us. Despite how legend depicts him, his real greatness lies in his day-to-day decisions that transformed Jewish life.[5] And he did not make them alone. The whole force of Rabbinic rhetoric and debate points toward a process involving many people.[6] In fact, Yochanan himself warns against a messianic fixation: "He [Yochanan ben Zakkai] used to say, 'If you hold a sapling in your hand and are told that the Messiah is about to arrive, first plant the sapling and then go out to receive the Messiah.'"[7]

As leaders, we are often surrounded by those who want us to be the Messiah, so much so that we sometimes want it for ourselves. But rather than focusing on Yochanan ben Zakkai's dramatic and charismatic escape, we should look at his daily decisions and his voice in the midst of debate. This is what keeps us humble; what keeps us human; what lets us build and work with others, to make mistakes at times, but to keep getting up. It's not messianic work, but it's holy.

Solidarity Ethnic and Human

Moses and Moral Responsibility

Rabbi Shai Held, PhD

Rabbi Shai Held, PhD, a theologian, scholar, and educator, is co-founder, dean, and chair in Jewish thought at Mechon Hadar, where he also directs the Center for Jewish Leadership and Ideas. He received the 2011 Covenant Award for excellence in Jewish education and teaches in synagogues and educational institutes across the United States and Israel. Rabbi Held holds a doctorate in religion from Harvard University and is an alumnus of the Wexner Graduate Fellowship and a faculty member of the Wexner Heritage Program. He has written *Abraham Joshua Heschel: The Call of Transcendence* and *The Heart of Torah*, a two-volume collection of essays on the Torah.

Genuine leadership is not (only) about technique; it is (also and primarily) about character.[1] Take Moses for example—the formative tale of his killing the Egyptian taskmaster tells us a great deal.

Upon witnessing an Egyptian beating a "Hebrew, one of his kinsmen," Moses intervenes, striking down the Egyptian oppressor (Exodus 2:11–12). When *we* encounter situations of injustice, we are more likely to pretend not to notice—or, when we do notice, to marshall a litany of rationalizations for remaining silent. Not so

Moses; in the face of injustice, he is characterologically incapable of callousness or complicity. And so he acts.

So far Moses acts *on behalf of* his kinsmen. But crucially, his circle of concern does not end there. After fleeing Egypt for Midian, Moses encounters local shepherds mistreating seven Midianite women and "rises to their defense, saves them, and waters their flock" (Exodus 2:17). The lesson is clear. The person chosen by God must not limit his outrage to injustices perpetrated against his own people; he must be incensed by—and must act against—injustice committed against *anyone*. Solidarity with one's own people is necessary, but not sufficient. Ethnic solidarity must be entwined with broader human solidarity. Only when Moses shows that he understands this lesson does God appoint him to lead the people out of the house of bondage (Exodus 3:10).

The verb describing Moses's intervention on behalf of the Midianite women is *vayoshian* (he saved them)—an anticipatory echo of God's own miraculous intervention at the sea, where "*Adonai* saved [*vayosha*] Israel that day from the Egyptians" (Exodus 14:30). Subtly, the Torah tells us that to side with the oppressed—whether Jewish or not—is to be like God. As God rebels against the oppression and degradation of the innocent, so too must God's appointed leader.

These parallel stories undermine the claims of hyper-particularism. To those who insist that "we should take care of our own and let others take care of theirs," the Torah responds with Moses, the leader whose example teaches that we rise to defend even those who are foreign to us.

But the Torah is careful to recount the taskmaster story first. As much as it is an error to imagine that lines of responsibility extend only to our family or kin, it is equally wrong to insist that they do not begin there. In Judaism's ethical ideal, the dichotomy between particularism and universalism is false and insidious—we are responsible both for our family and for the stranger. But of the two, the family is first. All too often in contemporary Jewish life, people feel that they must choose: we have to care for our own, *or* we have to care for everyone. But Jewish ethics is clear: we have to care for our own, *and* we have to care for everyone.

How did Moses learn to empathize with "the other," with the victim who is not his kin? Perhaps he learned to care by having been similarly cared for. The chapter we have been considering begins, after all, with the fascinating story of Pharaoh's daughter saving the infant Moses from the Nile: "[Pharaoh's daughter] opened [the basket] and saw that it was a child, a boy who was crying. She had compassion for him and said, 'This must be a Hebrew child'" (Exodus 2:6). Having cast the Israelites as a dangerous enemy, a potential fifth column that would one day undermine his rule, Pharaoh had called for a genocide of all Israelite boys (Exodus 1:22). But this young woman, Pharaoh's daughter, sees not an adversary but a child.

Note carefully how the text speaks. In general, the Israelites are described as "Hebrews"—the normal way for the Torah (or its characters) to emphasize their "otherness," from the people(s) around them.[2] Pharaoh's daughter understands that Moses is such a Hebrew, but she sees also that this Hebrew, this foreigner, is crying, and she is stirred by a sense of shared humanity to save him.[3] Moses, the Torah's paragon of human solidarity, is himself given life by an Egyptian woman's discovery of human solidarity.

Like the God he serves, Moses will not tolerate persecution, neither of Israelites nor of anyone else. But at the heart of his teaching is another insistence as well: just as God will not tolerate oppression *of* Israelites, God will also not abide oppression *by* Israelites. Just as God "hears" (*vayishma*) the cries of the Israelites moaning under Egyptian bondage (Exodus 2:24), so also will God "assuredly hear" (*shamo'a eshma*) the cries of widows and orphans abused by those more powerful than they (Exodus 22:21–23). Similarly, harassment or abuse of the stranger—the outsider who dwells with the Israelites—is an unendurable affront to God (Exodus 23:9; Leviticus 19:33–34; Deuteronomy 10:18–19). "God's people must not show any sign that they are becoming like the Egyptians ... in how they treat others, whether fellow Israelites or aliens living among them."[4]

So often, people in positions of leadership are tempted to go along to get along; to limit or even obliterate their ethical horizons; to remain silent and (thereby) to become complicit. As a counterweight to these all-too-human temptations, the Torah portrays a God who loves the stranger (Deuteronomy 10:18) and tells of Moses, the servant of this God (Deuteronomy 34:5), who will not—who *cannot*—countenance oppression anywhere. The greatness of Moses is a challenge and a goad—to care for our own and for the foreigner, and to resist the urge to choose one instead of the other.

▲▼▲▼▲▼▲▼▲▼▲▼▲▼▲

The Moral Mandate of Community

Dr. Yehuda Kurtzer

Dr. Yehuda Kurtzer is the president of the Shalom Hartman Institute of North America and a leading thinker and author on the meaning of Israel to American Jews, the value of the Jewish past to the Jewish present, and questions of leadership and change in American Jewish life. He received his doctorate in Jewish studies from Harvard University and an MA in religion from Brown University and is an alumnus of both the Bronfman Youth and Wexner Graduate Fellowships. Among his publications is *Shuva: The Future of the Jewish Past*, which explores tensions between history and memory, and ways to relate meaningfully to our past without returning to it. He lives in New York with his wife, Stephanie Ives, and their three children.

The gap between learning leadership and exercising leadership is immense, and the discovery of what it is actually like to lead change—the painstaking, laborious work of making headway one day while slipping back the next—is probably like experiencing a medical residency after years of learning how to be a doctor from books.

I learned great Torah leadership from my teachers in the Wexner Graduate Fellowship Program, often feeling that I was learning something I never fully appreciated, much less even knew existed. I still have a few favorite tidbits, most of them from Marty Linsky:

- Leadership is about disappointing your people at a rate that they can absorb.
- The difference between "adaptive" and "technical" change is often the instructive difference between good leadership and effective management.
- Leadership is a noun but not an abstraction; it can only be captured in the ongoing activity of making and remaking.
- Most of all—best of all—that leadership is a fundamentally subversive activity.

At the heart of it all was a different idea of leadership: the assumption that great organizations, companies, and institutions have strong individual leaders at the top. There are, no doubt, exceptions, but overall that is probably true; certainly anecdotal evidence bears it out. And there are, by now, several major interventions seeking to populate the top of the organizational food chain with appropriate talent to address this central concern. Leadership Torah, in other words, needs empowered enactors.

But I fear that this model of "strong leader at the top" can easily become a setup for moral failure. We are well schooled by now in spectacular moral failures by those very people whom we had thought to be great leaders—in part, precisely because of the great divide between the "great leader" and the people he or she was meant to be leading. The brilliance of leadership well exercised, so clearly differentiated from the ordinary stuff of organizational perpetuation and other forms of treading the institutional water, sows the seeds of its own undoing if it highlights the agency of the leader but downplays the capacity of the community to chart its own moral direction.

There is a fundamental flaw in vesting leaders with high expectations and the power to achieve them while assuming that those leaders will know how to moderate their power with the sense of moral responsibility that we expect of them. We end up elevating leaders to "greatness" and trusting—or hoping—that good moral judgment will just naturally emanate from them. What we discover is that our inflated expectations of greatness suppress whatever ethical urges the leader may bring to the task. We make the mistake of displacing the responsibility for the ethical from the community onto our mythically perceived leaders, who then do not exercise it responsibly.

What if, instead, we considered power and moral responsibility as two mutually interdependent and conditional categories? What if we conferred them as privileges to leaders only if they exercise the former in the service of the latter? This would require two course corrections to the current system that so often translates into scandal: recognizing that "moral meritocracy," and not just leadership skills, constitutes a requisite path to leadership; and, more importantly, cultivating the moral fabric of our communities from which the power of a leader derives and to which any leader is ultimately accountable. The leader-community relationship would be rooted in an explicit covenant, with the values of the community at its core. Communities would be in a position to reel in leaders who go astray long before they can commit the kinds of iniquity that bring them down. They would never get to the point of wielding the kind of power that makes it difficult to hold them accountable.

Leaders should not be charged with crafting and exclusively policing the moral obligations that properly belong to the community. They should instead be exemplars of the community's shared values and moral frameworks, from which they are chosen and to which they are held accountable. Instead of "With great power comes great responsibility," we should be saying, "There is no power without moral responsibility"; any claims otherwise are narcissistic pretensions.

These two stances transform our answer to the question, When a leader fails morally, who is accountable, the individual or the enablers? In the first model, responsibility falls on the leader, whose exercise of morality follows from a kind of naive communal trust in benevolence. While we might hope that we have done enough along the way to set the person straight, the best we can do is hope (on the other end) that they will not disappoint us. In contrast, when power is granted conditionally by a morally responsible community—be it a synagogue, a board, a network of peers, or a professional association—accountability for the moral behavior of the leader lies with those from whom the leader's power is derived. There is nowhere for a morally responsible community to hide.

In the former model, all we do is remove the failed perpetrator, sweep the issue away, and then try again with the same failed model in place. In the latter, the moral failures of our leaders make us revisit the structures of accountability that we have created. There is no escape from the painful process of rethinking, remaking, and purifying the infrastructure that allowed the leader to fail in the first place. This kind of adaptive change is long overdue, especially in a Jewish community that lives and dies on its effectiveness to compete for the affection of its members and can no longer hold people hostage to an identity that this free society enables them to jettison at will. We are meant to be the people of justice and righteousness, a mantle owned not just by our leaders but by us all. How we assign power to fulfill this mission is a massive moral opportunity for the Jewish People.

The Global Wrap of *T'fillin*

Touching Our Heart but Reaching the World

Rabbi Asher Lopatin is a Wexner Graduate Fellowship alumnus (V), and is president of Yeshivat Chovevei Torah Rabbinical School, a Modern Orthodox yeshiva committed to training Orthodox rabbis to serve the entirety of the Jewish community. He is married to Rachel Tessler Lopatin, also a Wexner Graduate Fellowship alumna (III); they met for the first time at a Wexner Institute. Rabbi Lopatin has *s'michah* from Rav Ahron Soloveichik and Yeshiva University, studied medieval Arabic thought (MPhil) at Oxford on a Rhodes Scholarship, and was the rabbi of Anshe Sholom Bnai Israel Congregation in Chicago for eighteen years.

There is something foundational about the laws of *t'fillin*. It is the only mitzvah commanded in the Torah four times, both before the Exodus from Egypt and the ensuing revelation and afterward. What makes *t'fillin* (this strange collection of parchment, leather boxes, straps, knots, and black paint) so important is the fact that they are coupled with the central story of our people (going from Exodus to the Land) and our central value as well, love of God. By wrapping *t'fillin*, we take this central story and value and then physically wear them on our hearts and heads.

So many other rituals are spiritual and esoteric; this one enables us to actually feel Torah and to feel its hold over us. It is thereby so essentially personal. Yet it also conveys the need to interact with the world around us. It is this dual role of personal ritual and public responsibility that makes *t'fillin* such a powerful symbol for Jewish leadership in our time.

T'fillin are made from two hard leather boxes, each one called (singular) *t'fillah*: the *t'fillah shel yad* (the arm *t'fillah*—literally, "hand" *t'fillah*, because it is tied in place around the hand) and the *t'fillah shel rosh* (the "head" *t'fillah*). Inside each is parchment upon which Torah verses relevant to the commandment to wear *t'fillin* are written. They are attached to the body by black leather straps.

The arm box is plain, lacking all external design. It is designed to fit on the upper arm so that it faces the heart when the person wearing it is praying. The laws demand that it be tied right over the skin with nothing intervening; a jacket or tallit, for example, goes over it, not under it.

The arm *t'fillah* is, therefore, the Jew's personal, heartfelt bond to God: something felt and experienced, privately, immediately, internally. It is called a "sign," as if it were actually inscribed upon the worshiper's skin—the way the "sign" of the rainbow, given to Noah, was written across the sky for all to see, not merely imagine. If you regularly wear *t'fillin*, you actually do develop a "*t'fillin* arm" for some time after it is worn because of the way it ties so tightly around you.

The second box is more elaborate. Its inside parchment contains the same verses but on four separate scrolls, each one placed in its own separate compartment but tied together with sinew-like strings. As opposed to the arm *t'fillah*, the head *t'fillah* has a fancy exterior that suggests (by external line drawing) or actually reveals the four compartments, pressed together; the ends of the strings that bind the scrolls appear outside the box.

The box fits over the wearer's head by a strap that circles the head, with the box going on the forehead, facing upward, but clearly visible for the world to see. The arm *t'fillah* is just a personal experience for the Jew who wears it—tied tightly next to the heart and covered by a sleeve or tallit. This head strap is worn like a crown, with the box being the crown jewel that radiates to all the world the joy, commitment, and purpose of being a Jew. The head *t'fillah* is not parochial or inward focused; it directs the Jew to think of himself or herself as a walking sanctifier of God's name. Everyone is meant to see the head *t'fillah*, which is to appear beautiful.

How we serve God and God's world can be gleaned by seeing the laws of *t'fillin* as our model. We first put on the arm *t'fillah* to develop an inward-focused, intense, and personal relationship with God, for in the end, it is we ourselves, each of us actually, whose personal commitment is at stake. But this intensely personal relationship with God is not enough, for Torah demands that we work publicly in God's world, not just privately in our own hearts. So we put on the head *t'fillah* as well, to focus us outward and avoid selfish insularity. Strengthened by inner commitment from the arm *t'fillah*, we now direct our self-confidence, purpose, and passion outward onto the world at large, to determine how, as both a Jew and a human being, we can influence and even re-create the world around us.

We need both *t'fillin*, because we cherish both the inner world of our heart and the outer world toward which the logic of our head directs us to take action. The "heart" *t'fillah* (so to speak) nourishes our personal spirituality, our relationship internally with God. Our "head" *t'fillah* sends us proudly into the world with the certain sense that we have something to contribute, something that we alone have to give to humankind.

No surprise, then, that *t'fillin* appear in the Torah around the Exodus from Egypt—the experience that sets us free in this world to change it. And no surprise also that *t'fillin* occur in the third paragraph of the *Sh'ma* itself, the prayer affirming the unity of God. To wear *t'fillin* is to experience this critical feature of Jewish leadership: to be directed by one's inner and spiritual passion but to express that passion in the world for which we were created.

▲ ▼▲▼ ▲▼▲ ▼▲▼ ▲▼▲ ▼▲

Look Out Above!

Keeping Values in Sight on Our Halachic Hike

Rabbi Daniel S. Nevins

Rabbi Daniel S. Nevins is the Pearl Resnick Dean of the Rabbinical School and the dean of the Division of Religious Leadership at the Jewish Theological Seminary of America. Previously he served as senior rabbi of Adat Shalom Synagogue in Farmington Hills, Michigan. As a member of the Committee on Jewish Law and Standards, he writes responsa (halachic opinions) on diverse topics of social significance and has published widely in books, journals, and news media. See www.rabbinevins.com for access to his work.

What is halachah (Jewish law)—an anchor to our ancient past, or a guide to a redemptive future? A system of crystallized rules, or a dynamic web of values? All of the above, but you wouldn't know it from the way that halachah is usually studied. Halachic investigation nowadays tends regularly but unduly to privilege the precedents of the past at the expense of the underlying values that we need for the future.

If I want to know whether an action is forbidden (*assur*) or permitted (*mutar*), demanded (*chovah*) or merely suggested (*r'shut*), then the appropriate first step is indeed to look for precedential guidance: the Bible, the Midrash, the Talmud; the great medieval codes of Jewish law and the vast corpus of halachic correspondence known as responsa. This first level of exploration focuses on *what* our ancestors said and did, not *why* they said and did it. Its great value is authenticity—if you follow in the footsteps of earlier generations, you are an authentic representative of the past.

This first step is often sufficient, but some questions are unprecedented and require a second step as well. Is it permitted, for example, to edit the human genome, permanently removing some features and permanently adding others? If you search through the Bible and Talmud, you will find nature-defying miracle stories like Joshua's stopping the sun in its tracks (Joshua 10:12–14) or Rabbi Eliezer's making a stream run backward (Talmud, *Bava Metzia* 59b). But you will not find proof that it is permitted or forbidden to edit the human genome in a way that alters the nature of humanity.

Faced with unprecedented questions, and no evidently relevant precedent, the halachist has two choices. She can declare freedom to do whatever she wants, or she can look below the surface to identify Jewish values that are expressed or even assumed by Jewish tradition and then integrate them into her contemporary halachic calculus. The first approach is formalist—it sees value in the system as already laid down—the Talmuds, the codes, the responsa, and the commentaries—and does not assign any legal role to considerations of morality or justice. The second approach is broader in that precedents are assumed to have underlying values that infuse the halachic system and can be drawn on for current challenges. These underlying halachic values—such as human dignity, humility, and compassion—become essential to halachic interpretation generally, but especially when there is no clear precedent to fall back on. The new ruling may not have precise precedent in practice, but it may still be continuous with the values that suffuse halachic literature.

In 2015, I wrote a responsum ("Halakhic Perspectives on Genetically Modified Organisms") that illustrates what I mean, in that I considered both precedent and values to formulate a religious response to the altogether new issues regarding the humanly engineered redesign of life. On the formal level, I asked whether the Torah's ban on mixing species (*kilayim*, see Leviticus 19:19) applies to the transfer of DNA segments from one organism to another, and I concluded that it does not. To arrive at the values, I posed certain moral and theological questions: Is the role of humanity to conserve God's creation or to perfect it? Doesn't our mandate to feed the hungry and to heal the sick require our using the remarkable tools of genetic engineering? Yet doesn't Judaism require humility in the face of the immense responsibility of reprogramming life? What is the line between "healing" and "enhancing" life, and what is the best strategy for preserving what is distinctive about human dignity? Jewish values were as important as legal precedents in my response to this novel question.

I have come to believe that values-based interpretation is equally important in areas of practice that are well precedented. Surely the purpose of praying, of observing Shabbat, or of keeping kosher is to make life holy—as the blessing states, *asher kid'shanu b'mitzvotav*, "God sanctifies us through the commandments." Under normal circumstances, no issues arise, but what about times when precedents and values are in conflict?

Take, for example, the tension between the strict observance of kashrut and maintaining relationships with family and friends who do not keep kosher. Someone who keeps kosher may not eat forbidden foods or dishes that mix dairy and meat. But we are obligated to honor our parents, and indeed to love all people, regardless of their personal practice of kashrut. What then shall we do when a person whom we love invites us for a meal that is not kosher?

Such a scenario calls for a response that does justice to the complexity of the case. It cannot be purely technical. Yes, we can consider formal aspects of the kashrut laws that support leniency, such as the annulment of forbidden substances with less than one-sixtieth of total volume (*batel b'shishim*). But we must also consider such halachic values as the obligation to honor parents, the ban on embarrassing others, and the importance of sanctifying God's name by explaining and exemplifying our religious commitments. Practitioners of halachah may be entitled, even obligated, to insist upon respect for the integrity of their religious practice, but the recognition of conflicting values can help defuse a situation and recognize the dignity of other participants.

It is a fallacy to assume that consideration of halachic precedent leads always to stringency, while the consideration of halachic values leads always to leniency. Often the results run in the opposite direction: an action may be formally permitted but incompatible with religious integrity. We need to "look out above," remembering our highest purposes in living a religious life: to show reverence for our Creator, to treasure our sacred tradition, to preserve our personal integrity, and to respect and love other people. When we do so, our halachic practice will guide us to walk upright with God, maintaining the covenant that is the anchor to our past and the key to our future.

▲▼▲▼▲▼▲▼▲▼▲▼▲▼▲

The God Who Loves Pluralism

RABBI RACHEL SABATH
BEIT-HALACHMI, PHD

Rabbi Rachel Sabath Beit-Halachmi, PhD, was ordained at Hebrew Union College–Jewish Institute of Religion (HUC-JIR) in New York, earned her PhD from the Jewish Theological Seminary of America, and is now national director of recruitment and admissions and President's Scholar of HUC-JIR. A Wexner alumna, she served for ten years also as vice president and faculty member of the Shalom Hartman Institute in Jerusalem, and for nearly thirteen years she was the rabbi at Congregation Shirat HaYam on Nantucket Island. Rabbi Sabath has published regularly in various academic and non-academic journals, co-authored two books, and written a monthly column ("Rethinking Judaism") for the *Jerusalem Post*. She is a recognized speaker, writer, and teacher in North America and Israel, on leadership, theology, Zionism, and gender.

The revelation at Sinai raised several core questions for Jewish thought, none of them more important than the twin issues of what the Torah means and who interprets it. Might there be more than one interpretation? How does God want us to study it?

These questions have been answered differently throughout time. Modern Jewish scholars as diverse as Abraham Joshua Heschel, David Hartman, and Judith Plaskow have noted that these questions are inherent in the ancient texts and Rabbinic interpretations themselves. Not only are there competing notions of authority and interpretation within the Bible, but the tensions between them have been retained—and should be retained—throughout the generations. Study and debate, it seems, are the primary ongoing and authentic Jewish responses to the revelation of God's word. God, one might even argue from the texts, desires the pluralism of the many possibilities that emerge from honest human, if sometimes differing, interpretations of divine law.

At the moment of the revelation at Sinai, it seems clear what Moses's role is supposed to be: "God called to him [Moses] from the mountain saying: Thus shall you say to the house of Jacob and declare to the children of Israel" (Exodus 19:3); and in a later section: "Write down these commandments, for according to them I make a covenant with you and with Israel" (Exodus 34:27). Moses, most traditional interpretations teach us, was a faithful servant and loyal scribe. But the sages of antiquity and the generations of commentators thereafter expand the human role significantly, to the point where we become much more than scribes. We become interpreters.

Abraham Joshua Heschel (1907–1972) devotes much of *Heavenly Torah* to unpacking the many approaches through which the sages sought to understand Torah and apply it to the life of a people. He demonstrates the multiplicity of interpretive schools—the veritable cacophony of voices and competing opinions that are intrinsic to the Rabbinic project.

Numerous Rabbinic texts emphasize the holiness of multiple interpretations. In a particularly long and intense argument between the House of Hillel and the House of Shammai, a "heavenly voice" declares, "Both these and those are the words of the living God" (Talmud, *Eruvin* 13b). God's ongoing revelation is apparently "big enough" to hold even contradictory ideas. In another famous argument where two rabbis go to extreme lengths to prove their respective opinions, God enjoys the debate enough to say, "My children have defeated me" (Talmud, *Bava Metzia* 59a–b). In the Jewish view of law, multiple interpretations not only can exist, they must—and then are celebrated as equally worthy of study. Seeking out the multiplicity of possibilities is precisely the interpretive act God wants.

David Hartman (1931–2013) emphasized ancient texts that model Rabbinic pluralism not only because he valued pluralism personally, but because he understood pluralism to be true theologically. One of his favorite texts pictures God seeking the capacity for pluralism in the human heart: "Make for yourself a heart of many rooms" (*Tosefta Sotah* 7:7). "In other words," says Hartman, "become a person in whom different opinions can reside together in the very depths of your soul.... Jewish tradition affirms an understanding of revelation in which God loves it when we discover ambiguity in God's word."[1]

While much of Jewish law seems to imply a single way to pray, keep kosher, or get married, these very same texts permit and even celebrate many voices and opinions. In tracing tradition's historical layers and interpretive approaches, we find that each generation determines anew who has the authority to interpret sacred texts and the possibilities as well as the limits of multiple interpretations. While each of us may wish to conclude that the correct interpretation is our own, we remain truer to the texts outlined above when we ask also what we lose if we fail to allow for the coexistence of "many rooms" of interpretations and ways of being Jewish.

This theology of pluralism underscores the way our textual tradition serves properly to underwrite Jewish leadership. We dare not minimize the significance of text—we are a textual tradition. But texts must be read, so our texts come bundled with interpretations that arise from the viewpoints of readers who necessarily bring to bear their own disparate lenses. Responsible Jewish life abhors the vacuum of any one particular view or community of practice; it demands constant challenges from rival points of view.

Jewish leaders need, therefore, to know and interpret text, and as we learned from Judith Plaskow (b. 1947), Jewish life is also richer if all women's as well as all men's interpretations are included. But we need also to have enough humility to imagine the possibility that other interpreters may understand revelation differently, and not altogether wrongly. "These and those are the words of the living God" now as much as in the time of the Houses of Hillel and Shammai. It is the very multiplicity of interpretation that contributes to the flourishing of the Jewish People and humanity as a whole.

As much as religious pluralism is celebrated, it is also constantly at risk. Jewish institutions—and the State of Israel itself—are often divided over the granting of authority to determine Jewish practice. Very rarely do leaders in such contexts argue for the possibilities of pluralism. But in fact the Jewish way is a continual affirmation of difference. In our essence we are an interpretive culture that acknowledges multiple understandings of Jewish tradition. If ancient Rabbinic culture itself celebrated multifaceted conversation, shouldn't we be wise enough to nourish that same pluralism and openness of heart in our time?

Leading from Tents, Not from Arks

Rabbi Joanna Samuels

Rabbi Joanna Samuels graduated magna cum laude from Barnard College, was ordained from the Jewish Theological Seminary of America, and is now executive director of Educational Alliance's Manny Cantor Center. Prior to joining Educational Alliance in 2012, she was the rabbi of Congregation Habonim in New York City. Her work at Advancing Women Professionals, furthering women's advancement and gender equity in the Jewish community, made her the first female rabbi honored by the Drisha Institute. Rabbi Samuels is a Wexner Graduate fellow, writes for local and national publications, and teaches at institutions throughout New York City. She serves on the advisory board of the West Side Campaign Against Hunger and lives in Manhattan with her husband and two children.

This year I celebrated my forty-fifth birthday and the thirteenth anniversary of my ordination as a rabbi. Of the two milestones, my bat mitzvah year as a rabbi loomed especially large. What have I given to the Jewish community and to the world? What have I done to make the highest use of the profound privilege of my education? What has my rabbinate amounted to, now no longer in its youthful glow?

I was blessed to have my bat mitzvah fall on Shabbat Noach, which juxtaposes two different structures: the ark (from the Torah reading, Genesis 6:9–11:32) and the tent (from the haftarah, Isaiah

54:1–55:5). "Ark," on one hand, and "tent," on the other, evoke two different strategies for moving a community forward.

The ark, of course, is what Noah builds at God's command: "God said to Noah: 'I have decided to put an end to all flesh.... Make yourself an ark'" (Genesis 6:13–14). So Noah does, without a single word of protest or response. He constructs a sealed and static enclosure in which to ride out the storm. While the world outside meets its watery death, Noah and his family and a menagerie of animals survive. Nothing less, but nothing more.

Eventually, God issues a second command, "Get out of the ark!" (Genesis. 8:16). But why did Noah need to be commanded? Surely, by then, he was sick and tired of the long voyage going nowhere—and in cramped quarters at that. A midrash explains that Noah held back because he feared that his descendants would defile the newly repurified earth, forcing God to send a second and final wave of destruction. God had to order him to leave.

The midrash is psychologically astute: it was easier for Noah to remain within the protective walls of the ark than to rejoin the world in which what was precious may well have been destroyed.

The same is true for us. How very tempting to build our own enclosures, with our handpicked companions. How very difficult to live with the chaos of heterodoxy. How frightening to think that we ourselves, released into the universe, might defile all that we and God hold dear—our communities, our projects, creation itself. How tempting it is to try to lead from the safety of an ark.

Nonetheless, it is tents that attract me, not arks. Arks have often ejected me, and I have often rejected them. Systems designed for self-protection and self-perpetuation—like Noah's ark—make me spiritually claustrophobic. When I am closeted away inside an ark, I become less generous, less kind, less aware of God's presence in my life. The problem with the ark is this: it divides the world into a binary of protection or destruction, abundance or scarcity, syncretistic dissolution or navel-gazing tribalism. So we cling, or we drift. Either way, we survive—but nothing more and nothing less.

I am, by nature, a tent dweller and tent builder—which brings me to the haftarah from Isaiah.

Isaiah commands a bereft and broken Israel, "Enlarge the site of your tent, / Extend the size of your dwelling, / Do not stint! / Lengthen the ropes, and drive the pegs firm" (Isaiah 54:2). What a contrast to Noah! Instead of "Enclose! Survive! Handpick your cohort! Leave only when forced!" the haftarah teaches, "Make it wider, extend it, be generous, stretch!" It is particularly powerful that these exhortations to remain open are given while in exile.

Isaiah also says of tents, "And drive the pegs firm" (54:2). A tent is open but also rooted, because as much as some people like the freedom to come and go at will, others require stasis, permanence, the sense of being grounded. Isaiah says also, "Enlarge the tent ... lengthen the ropes" (54:2). You cannot do that with an ark. When I imagine stretching the sides of a tent, I imagine having room for both sorts of people. No single sort has a definitive claim on my identity or the right to be part of our complex and multifaceted community. I trust our strength in diversity; I trust our porousness.

There is a famous and wonderful story about Mr. Rogers, who said, "When I was a boy and I would see scary things in the news, my mother would say to me, 'Look for the helpers. You will always find people who are helping.'"

The news is filled with scary things—there is no shortage of statistics and trends that foretell a dire Jewish future. But our Jewish tent has strong stakes in the ground with plenty of give in the fabric. So to paraphrase Mr. Rogers, I look away from the ark and toward the tent, with all its many kinds of helpers. Tents are designed for growth, for coming and going, for mixing and mingling, for taking risks, and for learning from one another. When I am plagued by questions about the Jewish future, I look to the people who are enlarging the tent—standing firmly while making our community broader and better. I try to be one of those leaders.

More places to be grounded and to stretch, fewer places to hunker down and ride out reality. More heterodoxies, fewer binaries. More dialogues, fewer survival narratives. More tents, fewer arks.

▲ ▲▼▲ ▲▼▲ ▲▼▲ ▲▼▲ ▲

Marshmallows, Ketchup, and Redemption

How Leaders Manage Expectations

RABBI JACOB J. SCHACTER, PhD

Rabbi Jacob J. Schacter, PhD, is university professor and senior scholar at the Center for the Jewish Future, Yeshiva University. He holds a PhD from Harvard University, has served as a pulpit rabbi for close to thirty years, is the founding editor of the *Torah Umadda Journal*, and has authored close to a hundred articles and two books, *A Modern Heretic and a Traditional Community: Mordecai M. Kaplan, Orthodoxy, and American Judaism* (co-authored with Jeffrey S. Gurock) and *The Lord Is Righteous in All His Ways: Reflections on the Tish'ah be-Av Kinot by Rabbi Joseph B. Soloveitchik*.

In a psychological experiment of the late 1960s and early 1970s, preschoolers were offered a choice between eating one marshmallow now or two marshmallows after waiting until the experimenter returned after a fifteen-minute absence.

Follow-up studies in what became known as the Stanford Marshmallow Experiment revealed that children who waited had better life outcomes: higher SAT scores, cognitive competencies, educational achievement, and more. Achieving good outcomes requires patience and the capacity to wait. Leaders too need to recognize that meaningful change takes time and patience.

You may remember the famous Heinz Ketchup commercial from the late 1970s showing children waiting—and waiting—for the ketchup to come out of the bottle. Carly Simon's song "Anticipation" played in the background, and the tagline at the end advertised "thick, rich Heinz Ketchup, the taste that's worth the wait."

What is the most famous question our kids ask us two minutes into a car ride? "Are we there yet?" It is a mark of maturity to recognize that getting "there" takes time.

Jews have not had to depend on marshmallows, ketchup, and car rides to learn this lesson. I am a firm believer that traditional Jewish texts provide meaningful leadership lessons, and this case is no exception. In the dialogue following God's directive to Moses to redeem the Jewish people from Egyptian servitude, Moses does everything he can to avoid the mission. And, at the end of a long conversation, he pleads, "Please, God, send whomever You will send [*sh'lach na b'yad tishlach*]" (Exodus 4:13). But God angrily ends the debate. Moses is to leave forthwith for Pharaoh's palace (Exodus 3:7–4:17).

I have three problems with this story. First, where is Moses's respect for God? God had sought out Moses, telling him explicitly that his efforts would succeed: "They *will* heed your voice" (Exodus 3:18). Yet, immediately thereafter, Moses insists, "They *will not* believe me; they *will not* heed my voice" (Exodus 4:1). How could Moses so blatantly and repeatedly reject God's will in an argument that, our Rabbis teach us, lasted for an entire week?[1]

Secondly, how can we understand the reluctance on the part of Moses to help his fellow Jews? After all, he was intimately familiar with what they were experiencing in Egypt, to the point of his having killed an Egyptian taskmaster many years earlier and having to flee for his life (Exodus 2:11–15). Why didn't Moses jump at the opportunity to return to Egypt with God at his side and redeem his sisters and brothers?

Finally, what is the meaning of this enigmatic plea, "Send whomever You will send [*sh'lach na b'yad tishlach*]"? Whom does Moses have in mind?

I once heard Rabbi Joseph B. Soloveitchik (1903–1993) address all three questions. He cited the midrashic work *Pirkei d'Rabbi*

Eliezer (chapter 40), which notes that Moses was referring here to Elijah the Prophet (question 3). "Don't send me," he told God. "Send Elijah." But why Elijah? And why did God peremptorily reject his proposal?

Knowing that Elijah was destined to be the harbinger of redemption, Moses argued, "I would happily do what You ask if I thought that the Exodus would lead immediately to the final redemption. But it won't. I know that if You send me, the Jewish people will first have to wander in the desert for forty years. Then even after we get to Israel, we will have to suffer the destruction of two Temples and go into a long and painful exile marked by tragedy after tragedy: the murder of the Ten Martyrs (second century); the Crusaders' massacre of Rhineland Jewry (eleventh century); more Crusader killing (twelfth century); the burning of the Talmud (thirteenth century); the Black Death Massacres (fourteenth century); the expulsion from Spain (fifteenth century); the Chmielnicki Massacres (seventeenth century); the Kishinev pogrom (twentieth century); the Holocaust (twentieth century); and then repeated acts of terrorism—buses blowing up on the streets of Jerusalem, rockets flying, yeshiva boys gunned down in front of their Gemaras, innocent people stabbed in synagogues and on the streets of Israel (twenty-first century)."

"What is the point," Moses continued, "of sending me now if, after me, You will anyway have to send someone else to usher in the final redemption? Why redeem Israel from slavery now if they will only be enslaved again and again and again? I beg You! Don't send me! Send Elijah and be done with it!" Moses showed God no disrespect (question 1). He just loved Israel so much that he wanted the messianic era to arrive immediately (question 2).

But God knew the lesson of patience. "Redemption doesn't work that way," God replied. "Yes, some day I will send Elijah (Malachi 3:23), but now I am sending you."[2]

Nothing profoundly good comes easily and immediately. Redemption, too, is not direct, straightforward, linear, unequivocal, automatic, and guaranteed. It is complicated, circuitous, and ambiguous. Redemption takes time. Redemption takes patience. Redemption is a process.

So is everything that we all do, for we too are part of this long march toward redemption. As leaders in Jewish life, we feel the need to push hard, very hard, to achieve our goals; we often feel that we do not have the luxury of patience. But we need to internalize God's lesson to Moses. All meaningful and lasting change is a process. We should not despair and disengage when the results we want are not as quickly forthcoming as we would like.

Extra marshmallows take patience. Ketchup takes patience. Long car rides take patience.

Jewish literacy takes patience. Jewish communal and religious engagement takes patience. Strengthening Jewish peoplehood takes patience. Ultimate redemption takes patience.

So we push ahead with full force but stay the course when the going gets rough. If we persevere over time, we will prevail. As Maimonides taught, "We are in possession of a divine assurance that Israel is indestructible and imperishable, and will always continue to be a preeminent community."[3]

The Voice at the Table

SUSAN K. STERN

Susan K. Stern is a local and national civic leader. Among other things, she has chaired the board of UJA Federation of New York and was the first woman national campaign chair for Jewish Federations of North America (JFNA). She is the former vice chair of the board of JFNA, a cabinet member of the American Jewish Joint Distribution Committee, and the immediate past chair of the New York State Commission on National and Community Service. In 2011 she was nominated by President Obama to chair the President's Advisory Council on Faith-Based and Neighborhood Partnerships, where she focused on the issue of human trafficking. She and her husband, Jeffrey, have two sons, Peter (married to Amanda) and Michael (married to Janna), and two grandchildren, Zachary and Alexandra.

As a child, I loved going to the synagogue and watching the rabbi end Shabbat services by raising his arms over the congregation and reciting the *Birkat Kohanim*, the Priestly Benediction. It always made me feel warm and protected, yet I never thought about what those warm and comforting words meant.

Over thirty years working as a volunteer in the Jewish community, primarily in the Federation world, these words fortify me when bureaucracy sometimes blurs the reason we do the work that we do. Very close to my own rabbi's translation is this one that I received from Rabbi Alyson Solomon:

> May God bless you and keep you.
> May the light of God's face shine upon you and bring
>   you grace.
> May God's face shine upon you and grant you peace.

I especially treasure the second line: "May the light of God's face shine upon you and bring you grace." These words frame for me the work we do in our philanthropic organizations. I learned from Rabbi Alyson Solomon their true meaning: "We acknowledge, appreciate, and seek to nurture the radiance of the faces of other people and bring their light into the world. To bless someone is to shine a spotlight of attention and care on them."

I have been privileged to travel the world and visit those we seek to bless in this way. They include individuals no one from our communities will ever meet or know but whose lives are touched and sustained by the decisions made every day by our organizations. Some are in our own backyard; others suffer constant war, anti-Semitism, or devastating poverty and the virtual absence of help from their governments. I rarely speak their language, but no matter: the tears in their eyes, the hugs that don't let go, and their implicit plea, "Please don't forget us," teach me the value of what we do.

With this privilege of visiting comes the responsibility to bring these recipients' stories to the tables where decisions are made. Yes, funds must surely be spent wisely and judiciously, but decisions to fund or defund cannot be based on business criteria alone. It is important also to have seen the work firsthand. Only by bringing the clients' stories into the discussion, and by "shining a spotlight of attention and care on them," do we fully comprehend that real lives with real consequences are at stake.

The importance of shining the spotlight on others was brought home to me many years ago by my son. Shortly after Operation Solomon, the rescue of fourteen thousand Ethiopian Jews to Israel in 1991, my husband and I brought our children to Israel to meet with newly arrived Ethiopian *olim* (new immigrants). We wanted our boys to understand the work we were doing. Our younger son, aged seven, began to play with Avi, an Ethiopian child of about the same age, who had lost his mother and whose father was too ill to make the airlift. Avi had followed his sister, who had seven children of her own, onto the airplane. He arrived in Israel literally with only the clothes on his back. Avi and Peter kicked around a soccer ball, communicating quite wonderfully without a common language. As we left and they were waving to each other, our son said, "We have to make sure Avi will be okay." He paused and looked at me and asked, "Is that what you do, Mom?" It was that question by a seven-year-old that reminds me regularly of my responsibility to the countless others in the world who, like Avi, have no voice but ours and need us to make sure they will be okay.

Many years later Gilad Shalit, the young Israeli soldier taken captive by Hamas, was finally released and asked to address a group in New York. This was the first time he had spoken publicly after six years in captivity, with little human contact. Overcome by the many people who had come to meet him, Gilad remarked that throughout his years in captivity, he hadn't realized that so much effort could be made for a single soldier. Shlomi Kofman from the Israeli Consulate responded tellingly: even though the people standing in that room had never met him, Gilad was our family; we had advocated, marched, and lobbied as if he were our own son. We were shining our light on him.

The beauty of Judaism is a tradition that often reminds us to take the role of the other, to imagine that we were once slaves in Egypt. That simple lesson has shaped my leadership over the years. By simple storytelling, by being the voice at the table, by shining a light on those we serve, we grasp the profound reality of what we do.

Leadership is many things, but part of it is helping decision makers attach faces and stories to impersonal facts and figures. It is to insist on seeing the human face of those who worry where their next meal will come from or who do their best to just survive but have the right to so much more. We need to be their voices to make sure their cries are heard. This is our sacred obligation.

▲ ▲▼▲ ▲▼▲ ▲▼▲ ▲▼▲ ▲

Judge Away

Rabbi Shira Stutman

Rabbi Shira Stutman is senior rabbi at Washington, DC's innovative Sixth & I Historic Synagogue, where she and her colleagues strive to create a spiritually connected, reflective, intellectually challenging, and engaging Jewish community for the area's large millennial population. When not at Sixth & I, Rabbi Stutman serves as the scholar-in-residence for the National Women's Philanthropy program of the Jewish Federations of North America, teaches for the Wexner Heritage Program, speaks nationally on a wide variety of topics, and is board chair of Jews United for Justice. She is a Wexner Graduate fellow.

The current pope is one of the more inspirational spiritual leaders of our time, but I was a little disappointed when, a few years ago, he was asked whether priests should be treated differently based on their sexual orientation. He answered, "Who am I to judge?"

Turns out—he's the *pope*. One of his responsibilities is to be a moral compass. The pope passes judgment all the time, as when he critiques the rich or when he chides governments for violent wartime campaigns. Leadership requires us to stand for and against, whether we're talking about marriage equality or murder.

Passing judgment is an integral part of the Jewish tradition. It is what inspires us to be activists in social change movements and to give *toch'chah* (reproach) when necessary. The Talmud teaches that we are so responsible for each other that if we have the opportunity to protest another's actions but do not, we will be held accountable for his or her misdeeds (*Shabbat* 54b–55a). Leadership is the willingness to take a stand on moral and ethical issues and to judge those who transgress.

While *judgment* is permissible and even necessary, *judgmentalism*, however, is not. Judgmentalism can be defined as forming an excessively critical opinion about another person based on unfair, unreasonable, unnecessary, or false rationales. (Beware sentences with the formula "all *x* are *y*.") Proper judgment attends to the issues at hand, weighing and measuring the arguments on both sides to arrive at a position we want to champion. Improper judgmentalism demonizes the opposition by overgeneralizing or by criticizing matters that we know too little about or that are not even our business in the first place. Judgment is responsible and born of objective truths and a moral code. Judgmentalism is dangerous and often born of bias and innuendo.

Tragically, judgmentalism has become something of a team sport in many Jewish institutions. We are judgmental of other people's political affiliations, observance levels, annual campaign gifts. This judgmental stance frequently starts at the very top—it is a norm that is actually modeled by institutional leadership, both lay and professional.

Ironically, even as we judge others, our own judgment typically is terrible. Study after study has demonstrated the prevalence of "confirmation bias," the human tendency to look for and assimilate information that confirms what one already "knows" to be true. We form our opinions (supporters of BDS are anti-Semites, civilians who own assault rifles are psychopaths) and then interact only with people and opinions that buttress those positions.

If we take as a given that human judgments are subject to fallibility, but also that making judgments is necessary, where does that leave us? Consider the Hebrew grammar construct known as *s'michut*. *S'michut* occurs when we take two nouns, change the vocalization slightly, and combine them, usually just to indicate possession, but sometimes to let the two words interact with each other to form a new idea. *Bayit*, "house," and *sefer*, "book," becomes *beit sefer*, "school." *Ooga*, "cake," and *g'vinah*, "cheese," becomes *oogat g'vinah,* "cheesecake." As a guiding principle, then: the next time you need to pass judgment, consider using *s'michut.* Combine your judgment with a generous helping of nuance, compassion, and curiosity, and get something different. Have clarity about the parts of the opposition's stand that you reject (exercise judgment), but couple it with the possibility that there may be additional parts of the story that you do not yet know (avoid judgmentalism).

A famous midrash illustrates what I have in mind:

> A king had some empty glasses. Said the king, "If I pour hot water into them, they will burst; if cold, they will contract [and snap]." What did the king do? He mixed hot and cold water and poured it into them, and they remained [unbroken]. "Similarly," said the Holy One, blessed be He, "If I create the world on the basis of mercy alone, its sins will be great; on the basis of judgment alone, the world will not exist. Hence I will create it on the basis of judgment and of mercy, that it may stand!"[1]

When we judge, we should do it—like God—in *s'michut.* When a colleague or congregant posts something we find repugnant, when a donor defaults on a pledge, even when an entire community takes up an incomprehensible (to us) political position, we should indeed give *toch'chah* (reproach), but only when we also eschew self-righteousness and engage humility. We ought never to forget that associated with *positions* are actual *people,* created in God's image, every single one. A bunker mentality based on separating ourselves from others, then deriding their opinions as instances of the bad people whom we imagine they must be, leads only to division and erosion of trust, even to war.

I am inclined to give the pope the benefit of the doubt, to assume that "Who am I to judge?" was his way of saying, "I refuse to be judgmental." His compassion and generosity of spirit imply his openness to reconsider the complexity of an issue that is rapidly evolving.

So may it be for us: may we stop defriending, disengaging, disinviting and instead reach out, ask thoughtful questions, push back. We are at a moment in history where the norm is to curate the ideas that we take in, being spoon-fed those that affirm our *rightness* and being shielded from those that challenge us. In the words of Nigerian novelist Chimamanda Ngozi Adichie, we must be wary of this, of the "danger of a single story." Yes, judge away, remembering that to live by a moral code has always been the Jewish path, but remembering too that only God knows the whole truth. To be one people, in all our fullness, we need to embrace a multiplicity of voices. God didn't merely create Adam and stop there. God knew that to be alone, with ourselves, our ideas, our lone perspective, was "not good." May our own judgment be strengthened, deepened, and made more just by the rich diversity of the Jewish People and by all of humanity.

Leadership and Confrontation

Lessons from Moses and God

Rabbi Melissa Weintraub

Rabbi Melissa Weintraub is the founding co-director of Resetting the Table, an organization that builds dialogue and deliberation across political divides on Israel in the American Jewish community. She was also the founding director of Encounter, an organization dedicated to strengthening the capacity of the Jewish People to be agents of change in resolving the Israeli-Palestinian conflict. Melissa received the Grinnell Young Innovator for Social Justice Prize, honoring demonstrated leadership and extraordinary accomplishment in effecting positive social change. An alumna of the Wexner Graduate Fellowship program, Melissa has lectured and taught in hundreds of forums on four continents. She was ordained as a rabbi at the Jewish Theological Seminary of America and graduated from Harvard University *summa cum laude*.

Jewish communal institutions that serve diverse constituencies—Federations, JCCs, Hillels, synagogues—inevitably face grueling junctures where their stakeholders grow bitterly divided around questions of boundaries and belonging. Who is given a platform and who barred? Who and what is counted, tolerated, celebrated, excluded, condemned? What is our institution's identity and role in a community divided over issues perceived as fundamental, even existential? Who gets to decide?

For the past decade, I have been involved in building institutional mechanisms and processes for difficult dialogue and deliberation across significant political differences in the American Jewish community around Israel. I have encountered several obstacles to repairing broken, fractious discourse in and across communities.

One is pervasive conflict avoidance. Institutional executives and boards often shut down controversy rather than "rock the boat," knowing that when controversies escalate they may risk withdrawal of funds, damaged reputations, and criticism from all sides. In working to smooth things over, however, leaders often neglect to address communal disagreements that simply will not go away. When your boat is already in turbulent waters, a "don't rock the boat" strategy represents a failure to help your community navigate through the storm.

Another obstacle arises when leaders facing contention around urgent, important decisions don't grant recognition to the legitimate concerns of those with opposing points of view. When "losing" parties feel slighted, voiceless, or disenfranchised—their positions excluded, dismissed, or even shamed rather than honored—the predictable result is a legacy of broken relationships, alienation, and fractured trust from which it can be difficult to recover.

The dialogue between Moses and God in the aftermath of the golden calf has much to teach us about overcoming these obstacles—and why it's worth it. Enraged over the people of Israel's consummate betrayal, God instructs Moses, "Let Me be, that My anger may blaze forth against them and that I may destroy them" (Exodus 32:10). Moses challenges God's directive, reminding God that God delivered this people from Egypt, made promises to their forefathers, and risks playing into the hands of those eager to declare the peoples' liberation a failed project.

A few crucial lessons emerge from their exchange.

One: *Leadership demands principled confrontation, so go there.* Moses doesn't shrink from the moment or pretend there's no issue. He doesn't try to placate God, minimize the problem, or change the subject. He knows there is a crisis that must be dealt with directly and in a way that honors everyone. He knows everything is on the line, but rather than fearing loss of status and position, he actualizes leadership by pushing back against the very Authority who has vested him with power. For the first time, rather than cowering before the role God has assigned to him—or acting as God's mouthpiece—he overcomes all hesitation and doubt to lead. It is a transformative moment not only for Moses, but for God. The Midrash sees God's words "Let Me be" as an implicit entreaty to do the very opposite: "Please don't let Me do this. Contend with Me; for this you have been created."[1]

Two: *In the course of confrontation, honor—don't shame.* In other words, *how* we confront one another matters more than the substance over which we argue. How does Moses confront God? Not by lashing out, but with love, and that is why he is able to effect change. He reminds God of God's own aspirations and standards, as if to say, "God, remember Your love for these people and how You want to be known. You would not be true to Your own ideals were You to cause them harm." This is what Martin Luther King Jr. did so well, every speech effectively proclaiming, "I am holding you up to your own values, America; your own standards of justice and holiness. I am helping you return to who you are and who you want to be."

Three: *When wielding power, heed the wisdom of those who challenge you.* This is especially important if your decisions could carry grave consequences and you might insulate yourself from critique. God could have rebuffed Moses by saying, "How dare you defy Me!" or "These traitors can never again be My people." Instead, despite having all the raw power to do otherwise, God listens, is instructed, and changes course. The problem remains; the people must be held accountable for what they've done, but not at the cost of letting a dark moment destroy the relationships and core mission to which God is committed. God models here the importance of owning our fallibility, an idea intensified by Rabbinic commentaries in which God claims that in learning from Moses, He wins, whereas had He won, He would have lost.[2]

This is by no means easy. Most of us discredit those who disagree with us out of hand, rather than opening our ideas to scrutiny or welcoming the kind of dialogue that just might change our minds. We imagine ourselves in the Moses role: trying to communicate messages that matter to those we see as clouded by anger, power, self-righteousness, or ideology. The truth is we are all Moses and God here: in need of learning how to fight for what matters to us and challenge one another with generosity of spirit; in need of learning how to welcome the challenges of others and step into each other's lenses and worldviews.

On issues inspiring passionate disagreement like Israel, we need more God-and-Moses dialogue:

- Going toward the heat, rather than avoiding it
- Naming and inquiring into our differences without demeaning our counterparts' ideas
- Taking in what others have to say and allowing it to stretch our own thinking
- Extending honor in our efforts at influencing each other's thinking: "Here's an opportunity to realize your own best self and true values."

These principles represent, as Moses found, the keys to effective persuasion. They also, as God models, present the risk—and opportunity—that just as we may challenge the judgments of others, so too we may need to revise our own. Our very survival as a people may hinge on our willingness to enter courageously into dialogue and allow ourselves to be changed.

▲ ▲▼▲ ▲▼▲ ▲▼▲ ▲▼▲ ▲

Keep It Simple

The Three Stages of Change

RABBI AVI WEISS

Rabbi Avi Weiss is founding rabbi of New York's Hebrew Institute of Riverdale–The Bayit and founder of Yeshivat Chovevei Torah and Yeshivat Maharat. He is also co-founder of the International Rabbinic Fellowship, an organization of Modern Orthodox rabbis, and is chair of the founding committee of PORAT–People for Orthodox Renaissance and Torah. Rabbi Weiss served as national chairman of the Student Struggle for Soviet Jewry from 1982 to 1991 and subsequently as national president of AMCHA–The Coalition for Jewish Concerns, raising a voice of moral conscience on behalf of the Jewish People and humankind throughout the world. He is the author of *Holistic Prayer*, *Women at Prayer*, *Spiritual Activism*, and *Open Up the Iron Door: Memoirs of a Soviet Jewry Activist*.

As I've grown older, I've come more and more to appreciate the simple over the complex. The truest and most profound ideas turn out to have been the simple ones. So, too, with leadership, the very core of which begins with identifying a need and responding to that need. In short, leadership is change. Here is the simplicity of it all: the three tried-and-true stages of change that every leader must encounter.

Stage 1: A Lonely Voice on the Fringe

Resistance to change is inevitable, first and foremost by the establishment, which is mired in bureaucracy and encumbered by red tape. The people most likely to see the need for change and then to initiate it are, therefore, those operating outside the mainstream, who need answer to no board or executive committee, and can operate more freely, courageously, and expeditiously.

Ever since biblical times, we see that pattern. Abraham himself began on the fringe, a lone voice promulgating monotheism against all odds. He is even called *ivri*, a person from "across [the river]." The whole world, say the Rabbis, was on one side of the river, and Abraham stood alone on the other.[1]

Consider, too, Moses and Aaron, who had persuaded the Jewish elders to join them on a freedom march to Pharaoh's palace. Yet, when the time came, says the biblical commentator Rashi, "One by one [the elders] dropped out. Only Moses and Aaron showed up."[2]

So too today: neither the American civil rights movement nor the anti–Vietnam War movement began in the mainstream; the struggle to free Ethiopian Jewry was for years the lonely cause of just the heroic Graenum Berger and a small number of activists; the Soviet Jewry movement was pioneered by visionaries like Jacob Birnbaum and Glenn Richter, who, by and large, stood alone.

Spiritual leadership has followed a similar pattern. In the early twentieth century, Sarah Schenirer (1883–1935), believing women could learn Torah, founded Bais Yaakov schools for women; Rabbi Meir Shapiro (1887–1933) instituted the *daf yomi* (the program of learning a page of Talmud daily); Rabbi Avraham Isaac Kook (1865–1935) insisted that religious Jews could combine Torah learning with defending Israel. When they first spoke, theirs were all lone voices.

Stage 2: Expect Establishment Opposition

Innovations require changing public policy that the establishment has consistently supported. Leaders who question that policy increasingly attract the vitriol of establishment opposition, no easy matter given the fact that the establishment controls the media and speaks with authority.

It is not easy to leave the tranquil mainstream and head toward turbulent waters; we are hardwired to join with the voice of the majority. As opposition mounts, it becomes tempting to retreat to the status quo ante. But a fundamental principle of leadership is to do what is right, even if it is not popular—and even when uncertain of victory: in short, to overcome humankind's natural resistance to taking risks.

So those who introduce new ideas often begin alone; but they cannot remain alone. One must navigate the inevitably choppy waters of a critical establishment and a reluctant public—including those who, in principle, believe in the cause but fear being ostracized if they dare to join in. Getting *everyone* on board is no easy feat.

Stage 3: Stay the Course; Demonstrate Success; Develop Followers

Buffeted by the waves of opposition, which can indeed become brutal at times, it is tempting to seek legitimacy from the detractors, but the key is not to waste energy on them. Instead, one must remain convinced of one's goal, to proactively move forward and garner eventual support by changing the facts on the ground.

Take activists for Soviet Jewry, for example. Only with determination and success did the mainstream—an embarrassed mainstream, actually—join the effort. The same is true of the movement for Ethiopian Jews.

Consider also today's widespread practice of women learning Torah; tens of thousands now study *daf yomi*. And many religious Jews play a central role in the IDF, defending the State of Israel. Neither cause was embraced early or easily by an establishment that just naturally resisted change.

Only when a cause acquires a measure of respectability will members of the establishment "boldly" step in, but they will distance themselves from, and even discredit, those who first stirred the conscience of the community. For the true leader, the once-lone figure now standing among the crowd, this should be of little importance. What counts is the cause, not the ego; the achievement, not the details of how it was reached.

In fact, followers play an equally important role in the success of a movement. A wonderful video called *Leadership Lessons from Dancing Guy* shows a young man dancing alone on a park hillside. Though he's hoping to inspire others to join him, he confidently dances alone. But after fifteen long seconds, a second dancer joins in. Only once a second person joins does the initiator become a leader.

In time, a third person joins the dance. But it's not the first dancer (the initiator, now the leader) who attracts him; it's the second dancer—the first follower, whose courage proves contagious. "First followers," especially, need to be nurtured because new followers emulate followers—not the leader.

Leadership is a symphony. Those who are there first unite with followers—who themselves become leaders, inspiring others to join in. And when many join in, you have a movement.

Ralph Waldo Emerson, said it well: "Do not go where the path may lead, go instead where there is no path and leave a trail." Successful leaders blaze a trail, inspiring others to join in the journey toward repair and redemption of the world.

"Let What Is Broken So Remain"

Leadership's Lotus Hour

Rabbi Mishael Zion

Rabbi Mishael Zion is rabbi and community scholar of the Bronfman Fellowships and a faculty member at the Mandel Leadership Institute and the Shalom Hartman Institute in Jerusalem. He is the author of *A Night to Remember: The Haggadah of Contemporary Voices*, the Israeli best-selling *Hala'ila Hazeh: The Israeli Haggadah*, and of the forthcoming *Megillat Esther: An Israeli Commentary*. He lives in Jerusalem with his wife, Elana, and three daughters, and he blogs regularly at "Text and the City."

No leader manages without some moments of despair; of dropping the gauntlet and limping off the scene in intense self-doubt. Moses, our teacher in all things, is our teacher in this moment as well. Hearing that Pharaoh has dispatched soldiers to arrest and execute him for killing the Egyptian taskmaster, Moses flees to Midian, where he sits wearily down "beside a well" (Exodus 2:15).

I try to imagine young Moses's internal monologue as he sits there in deep despair. His first foray into "leadership" has back-fired. Just a few verses ago he "grew up, and went out to his kins-folk and witnessed their labors" (Exodus 2:11). He saw—and took action! Isn't that what leaders are supposed to do?

But somehow now, he is a murderer, despised by Israelites and Egyptians alike. His adopted father has put a price on his head. Alone beside the well, Moses probably has no intention whatever of going down the activist's path again.

In my imagination, Moses's Midian is Homer's Odyssian "Island of the Lotus-Eaters," the narcotic haven where Odysseus's sailors eat the lotus and lose all desire to continue their journey home. As Tennyson puts it in his poem "The Lotos-Eaters":

> Most weary seem'd the sea, weary the oar,
> Weary the wandering fields of barren foam.
> Then some one said, "We will return no more";
> And all at once they sang, "Our island home
> Is far beyond the wave; we will no longer roam."...
> Let what is broken so remain.
> The Gods are hard to reconcile:
> 'Tis hard to settle order once again.

In Midian, Moses tastes the lotus and declares, "Let what is broken so remain." For all intents and purposes, he plans on staying there forever, becoming a simple shepherd and leaving his leadership career behind him. But then something surprising happens:

> The priest of Midian had seven daughters. They came to draw water, and filled the troughs to water their father's flock; but shepherds came and drove them away. Moses rose to their defense, and he watered their flock. (Exodus 2:16–17)

Harassed by local shepherds, the young women need a savior. Despite himself, Moses finds himself stepping up again. The key Hebrew word here is *vayoshian*—not just "Moses rose to their defense" but, more literally, "Moses rose up and delivered them." Just as Pharoah's daughter once delivered him from the Nile, just as God will soon deliver the Israelites from Egypt (with Moses in the lead). Yes, Moses is still young, and he has made his share of mistakes, but the incident of the Midianite women reminds him that he is a deliverer. It'll take many decades and a vigorous shaking up from God at the Burning Bush for that lesson to be internalized. But it will be. Eventually, Moses will rise to the task and deliver his people from Egypt—and with them give the world the greatest story ever told.

According to local legend, the site of Homer's lotus-eaters is identified as the Tunisian Island of Djerba. How ironic, then, that the most stirring teaching about Moses's young leadership comes from Djerba. Rabbi Moshe Chalfon HaCohen, the early twentieth-century leader of the Djerba Jewish community, turns Midian from a lotus-eating island resort into the exemplar of moral leadership for generations.

Chalfon reveals a symbolic arc to young Moses's saving interventions. It all begins with leaving the palace to "see the situation" with his own eyes (Exodus 2:11). He then attacks the Egyptian who was beating a Jew (2:12), but immediately thereafter he intervenes in a fight between Jew and Jew (2:13); and then he saves the seven daughters of the Midianite priest, Jethro, from the hand of shepherds and robbers (2:17). From intentional observation, Moses progresses from (1) non-Jew versus Jew, to (2) Jew versus Jew, and then (3) non-Jew versus non-Jew.[1]

Chalfon draws the following lesson:

> All people of open heart and righteous spirit must learn from Moses to take a stand and deliver their brethren from the hand of those who exploit them. This is especially true in those places where our brothers are oppressed and tormented by those of "no covenant."
>
> However, even if one of our fellow Jews is exploiting others—one cannot turn a blind eye. Action must be taken to help rescue the oppressed. Even when the oppressed person is not of our faith, it is proper that even in such a situation one stand in support of those who are being persecuted, because "*any* oppressor is repulsive to God" (Deuteronomy 25:16).[2]

Like Moses, our obligation is to stand up for the rights of the oppressed, regardless of their religion, nationality, or citizenship.

Chalfon's universalist stance, it is important to note, is rooted in his particularistically Jewish identity. As Chalfon describes it, Moses's initial sense of justice arises from a concern for other Jews. Only after learning the moral lesson "at home" (so to speak) does the subsequent universal mission crystallize. Concern for my "brothers" doesn't make me blind to the world; rather, it trains me for it.

In a world where the lotus entices us more than ever to "let what is broken so remain," I find comfort in the fact that even Moses, our greatest leader, gives in for a moment. But may my portion be along the path of moral leadership described by Rabbi Chalfon. We all have moments of doubt and darkness; but we all can aspire to get up and rise up in support of fellow brothers and sisters, and in support of all who are being persecuted, because "*any* oppressor is repulsive to God."

PART TWO

The Jewish Condition

▲

The Global View

Why Programs in Leadership? Why Now?

A Historical Perspective

Dr. Robert Chazan

Dr. Robert Chazan serves as Scheuer Professor of Hebrew and Judaic Studies at New York University, where he was founding chair of the Skirball Department of Hebrew and Judaic Studies and now co-directs the Programs in Education and Jewish Studies and the Wagner-Skirball Dual Degree Program. He has written many books on medieval Jewish history, as well as numerous articles for various publications. His two most recent books are *The Jews of Medieval Western Christendom* and *Reassessing Jewish Life in Medieval Europe*. He served as chairman of the Wexner Graduate Fellowship Committee from its inception through its first twenty-five years.

Jewish life over the ages has been graced by a sequence of powerful leaders: Abraham, Moses, David, Isaiah, Ezra, Judah the Maccabi, Rabban Yochanan ben Zakkai, Rabbi Judah Hanasi, and Rabbi Moses ben Maimon (Maimonides), to name but a few. Interestingly, the foundations of their authority have varied considerably. The reason that these leaders were accepted by their followers—why their authority was acknowledged—has evolved with the passage of time.

The earliest of the leader figures—Abraham, Moses, David, and Isaiah—are portrayed as appointed directly by God, divinely chosen for their diverse roles. With Ezra, the basis for Jewish authority shifted. Ezra is portrayed differently. Rather than being empowered directly by God, his mandate to lead derives from the fact that he commands the record of God's revelation to Israel. It is only with Ezra that we hear of that record coalescing into a sacred book, which Ezra reads to all the people (Nehemiah 8:1–8), as the core of his authority.

Command of this Written Torah and, eventually, the right to interpret it (the Oral Torah as well) constituted the foundation of authority for the next stage of Jewish leadership—the Rabbis. Throughout the Middle Ages, rabbinic leadership grounded in Torah remains, but we also learn of a separate group of leaders in Jewish communal life—leaders whose power was rooted in the reality of their economic prowess and their connections to the non-Jewish rulers who, in the final analysis, controlled the Jewish community and its affairs.

A few hundred years ago, however, Jewish life underwent a massive transformation as a by-product of the overall restructuring of Western societies in accord with Enlightenment ideals. Newly modernized Western states offered Jews *as individuals* all the opportunities attendant upon full citizenship in the body politic, and with that the premodern segregation of Jews into a semi-autonomous and self-governing corporation came to an end. With this momentous transition, leadership in the Jewish world was irrevocably altered. Among religiously traditional Jews, the historical authority of the rabbis as experts in Jewish law was retained. But new forms of Jewish religious life and identity entailed innovative forms of rabbinic leadership—people still called "rabbi," but with leadership claims based on foundations other than their traditional competence at applying Talmudic law to Jewish life. More striking still, this post-Enlightenment revolution created patterns of Jewish organization that went beyond religion altogether, requiring forms of Jewish leadership having nothing to do with religious competence. Inevitably, there arose the question of why

Jews should accept the dictates of these new-style leaders. What are the grounds of their authority?

This ongoing radical change in the organizational structures of Jewish life and in the nature of Jewish leadership it has entailed has led to the enormous interest in nurturing Jewish leaders for our time. Altogether new today is our sophisticated inquiry into the modalities of leadership training. As before, even in premodern times, some leaders still derive authority from their undisputed economic and political power or (if they are traditional rabbis) from their expertise in Torah. But contemporary Jewish life demands more. We now require leaders who are recognized and accepted for a range of leadership qualities—knowledge in any one of multiple domains, leadership skills, and personality traits—that can be developed and fostered. American Jewish leaders increasingly receive training that enriches their knowledge, develops their leadership skills, and burnishes those personality traits that make for effective leadership.

In addition, we are discovering that bringing American Jewish leaders together into regular contact with one another in and of itself provides reinforcement and improvement of leadership qualities. The premodern unity of the Jewish world has been irrevocably lost. Given the fracturing of American Jewry into multiple religious denominations, ideological perspectives, and organizational objectives, it becomes enormously important to provide opportunities for the many diverse leadership groupings to engage one another informally and comfortably, so as to foster mutual respect for one another and to mitigate needless conflict among them.

The traditional structures of Jewish communal life have been altered, and leadership patterns have changed radically as a result. The focus on American Jewish leadership is becoming an entirely new field, in no small part owing its centrality to The Wexner Foundation, which has so successfully fostered it. Leadership study and training are advancing the creation of new leadership patterns and the emergence of more effective American Jewish leaders.

▲▽▲▽▲▽▲▽▲▽▲

Three Eras of Jewish History and Their Leaders

Rabbi Irving (Yitz) Greenberg

Rabbi Irving (Yitz) Greenberg has served in the rabbinate, in academia, and as a Jewish communal professional. He is a covenantal theologian who has written on post-Shoah theology, pluralism, Jewish-Christian relations, and the ethics of Jewish power. He is the author of *The Jewish Way, For the Sake of Heaven and Earth: The New Encounter of Judaism and Christianity*, and most recently, *Sage Advice: Pirkei Avot — A New Edition and Commentary*.

Dor dor v'dorshav: each generation, says the Talmud, has its own distinctive teachers and leaders. It helps also to correlate leadership not just with generations but with eras, of which Jewish history has three. The third is currently under way. Each era has its own distinctive leaders, institutions, and understanding of God (from whom stems the Jewish mission in the first place).

Era 1: The Bible

In the biblical era, the central challenge was to gain a homeland and create a society that could live up to Israel's distinctive moral/religious code, the Torah. Changing circumstances produced three sets of leaders: political, religious, and prophetic. By political, I mean the judges who conquered the land, but then the monarchy, chosen when judges could not cope with invading sea peoples, the Phoenicians, whom the Bible calls Philistines. Centralized royal power enabled the construction of a national sanctuary with a priesthood—the second set of leaders—whose major contribution was to develop the Torah's vision of life against death and then develop an ethos of choosing life through the cult's demands for ritual purity and ethical behavior.

For some time, kings and priests, monarchy and cult, functioned jointly in effective symbiosis, each one needing the other. But the rise of world powers like Egypt, Assyria, and Babylonia broke the synthesis. Israel's kings were not nimble enough to negotiate Jewish independence while playing off the mega-powers of the time. Domestically, they failed doubly. They capitulated to the seduction of pagan religions, and they exploited their own people. Betrayed by corruption and incompetence, the first Jewish commonwealth and its Temple were destroyed, and the people went into exile.

The third set of leaders saved the day—the prophets who upheld the covenant, denounced pagan influence, and insisted that God wanted justice for all and help for the downtrodden. They predicted that divine rejection of the systemic immorality and exploitation would bring retribution—as indeed it did, with the sanctuary's destruction and exile. Most of those carried away were lost to Jewish history. But the catastrophe convinced a remnant that the prophets' message had been valid. They repented and renewed the faith. Eventually, they returned to build a second commonwealth and Temple, rooted in covenantal standards.

Era 2: The Rabbis

That commonwealth and Temple were eventually destroyed by another world power, Rome. But the second era had already begun with the rise of the Rabbis. God, the Rabbis taught, had self-limited in shaping the course of history—no more prophets, heavenly voices, and miraculous events like splitting the Red Sea. Instead, human understanding, analysis, and discussion rooted in Torah would discern God's will and guide the body politic. When leaders would act wisely, God would help behind the scenes—as in the story of Purim. When they fell short of such wisdom, they suffered the consequences—as in the reckless revolt against Rome, where Jews were crushed.

From that defeat, there emerged the new challenge of maintaining identity as a minority, generally as strangers in a strange land, to uphold the Jewish mission and sense of election in the face of persecution and pariahdom. Rabbinic leaders constructed an all-encompassing religious culture that enriched life and kept the hope of redemption alive. They made Torah study and education the birthright of everyone. Thus did Jews internalize the message of the covenant and remain Jewish even in adversity.

Jewish lay leaders followed the rabbis, avoiding the temptation to revolt against their national or regional hosts and negotiating space for Jews to stay cohesive. With God allowing greater human autonomy, Jewish leadership expanded from genetically designated priests to a meritocracy, based on learning, teaching, and service. With God hidden, there could be no Temple of visible Presence in Jerusalem, but holiness could be uncovered everywhere through Torah and ethical behavior. Instead of a national Temple and sacrificial cult, the rabbis developed the localized synagogue and rituals of prayer.

This coherent rabbinic system lasted almost two millennia, but it required a certain degree of Jewish separatism. It was undermined, therefore, by the arrival of modernity, which invited Jews to accommodate to the point of becoming like everyone else, pursuing *tikkun olam* (repairing the world) but without remaining outsiders. The second era survival strategy finally collapsed when the Holocaust demonstrated that the policy of political accommodation was bankrupt. Jews required their own homeland once again. In the postmodern era, no distinctive group can survive without their own power of sovereignty.

Era 3: Lay Judaism

The Holocaust only underscored just how much God had self-limited in history. In postmodernity, God became more hidden, allowing the creation of a scientific worldview that admits no manifest or detectable presence of the Divine. God must be encountered as that which instills the characteristics of matter and sustains the laws of nature—and calls on humans to use scientific knowledge as God's covenantal agents in repairing the world.

The central challenge of this period is twofold: (1) to build an independent homeland where Jews can live in dignity and peace while developing their own culture and society with covenantal purpose and standards; and (?) to develop a religion and culture magnetic enough to inspire loyalty in a world where Jews—and all people—are free to choose their identity and where competitive lifestyles and worldviews abound.

In Israel, the problem of identity is temporarily solved by living as the majority in a predominantly Hebrew culture. In the Diaspora, however, we have no such luxury. So far, at least, our inherited leaders and institutions are too anchored in the second era—still presupposing Jewish pariahdom or persecution, or so parochially Jewish, religious, and particularistic that Jews fully integrated in postmodernity hesitate to go there.

Jewish leadership today will necessarily be more secular, in line with a world called to secular holiness by God's self-limitation in history and the divine invitation to humans to complete *tikkun olam*. Israel is run by Knesset members, generals, and civil servants who need not be religious yet who understand that in the end, matters of state, although secular in nature, must meet covenantal standards. Their Diaspora equivalents are philanthropists, business leaders, communal professionals, and lay activists. In both places, rabbis play a role only if they too can function in secular settings.

Yet however much these leaders may be secular problem-solvers, their ultimate goal remains religious, for their raison d'être is still the charge to enrich Jewish identity, incarnate the covenantal mission, and hammer out the values that make being Jewish worth the effort.

The new era is barely under way. In the Diaspora, at least, we are engaged in a race between leadership development and communal revival, on one hand, and rising assimilation, on the other. The race's outcome will determine whether the Jewish mission will continue for another millennium.

I want to acknowledge and celebrate the pioneering role played by Leslie Wexner and Herb Friedman, who discerned that a revolutionary situation demanded new leadership and institutional transformation. They saw particularly the need to identify, educate, and inspire lay leadership not just in leadership skills but in the Jewish life and values that must underwrite their efforts. Their vision has enhanced our chances of winning the race. But the outcome remains uncertain, the task is unfinished, and the future is in our hands.

The Jewish People's Story, Not Just My Own

Dr. Deborah E. Lipstadt

Dr. Deborah E. Lipstadt, Dorot Professor of Modern Jewish and Holocaust Studies at Emory University, has written six books, including *History on Trial: My Day in Court with a Holocaust Denier*, which recounts her libel trial in London against David Irving, who sued her for calling him a Holocaust denier. The movie *Denial*, based on her trial, is due for release in 2016. She was a historical consultant to the United States Holocaust Memorial Museum, was appointed by Presidents Clinton and Obama to the Holocaust Memorial Council, and represented President George W. Bush at the sixtieth anniversary of the liberation of Auschwitz. She holds honorary degrees from various institutions, among them Hebrew Union College–Jewish Institute of Religion, Yeshiva University, and the Jewish Theological Seminary of New York.

What follows is a story—not just my own, but of all Jews, an exemplary account of a time when a variety of leaders worked together behind the scenes for the benefit of us all. I have told it in greater detail elsewhere but include it here as a model of how many people working together can accomplish what no person can do alone.

The story begins in 1995, when David Irving, then arguably the world's most prominent Holocaust denier, sued me for libel.

In my book *Denying the Holocaust: The Growing Assault on Truth and Memory*, I had described him as a "Hitler partisan wearing blinkers" who "distort[ed] evidence ... manipulat[ed] documents, [and] skew[ed] ... and misrepresent[ed] data in order to reach historically untenable conclusions." I wrote that "on some level Irving seems to conceive himself as carrying on Hitler's legacy."[1]

Irving was particularly dangerous in that (unlike other deniers) he had authored numerous books about World War II and the Third Reich. The fact that they were reviewed in major periodicals might lead people to wonder if there was any truth to them.

At first I did not take Irving's threats seriously. My sources were all documented. I had invented nothing. Irving gave speeches promising to "sink the battleship Auschwitz." He asked a survivor how much money she had made having a number tattooed on her arm. I dismissed his legal threat as a publicity-grabbing maneuver.

But Irving pursued his case. Moreover, British law placed the burden of proof on me as the defendant. I had to prove I told the truth. If I did not fight back, he would win by default, making it illegal to call Holocaust denial into question. Yet what could I, one single person, do?

Enter, here, the Jewish People.

To begin with, friends in the United Kingdom led me to a lawyer, Anthony Julius, renowned as Princess Diana's divorce attorney, but a specialist in libel law, a PhD in comparative literature, and the author of a book chronicling T. S. Eliot's overt anti-Semitism and the reluctance of critics to condemn Eliot for it. Anthony had taken on two British icons, the House of Windsor and T. S. Eliot, and won. He agreed to represent me "*pro bono* if necessary." I relaxed for the first time in months.

But the case grew steadily in intensity and scope, forcing Anthony to conclude that *pro bono* was no longer an option. I would need money to cover costs. Anthony's projected budget arrived as I was leaving for a Wexner Heritage seminar. I turned to the last page and blanched. The bottom line: $1.6 million.

As word of my predicament spread at the seminar, other allies appeared, not just friends in the United Kingdom, but Rabbi

Herbert Friedman, president emeritus of The Wexner Foundation, who asked how I was planning to raise the money. I admitted to being clueless. For me, Friedman's response was memorable. "It's time to get organized," he said clearly. "Irving set his sights on you, but it's the entire Jewish community that he is aiming at." As an academic, I was used to working on my own. Friedman knew that here that would not suffice.

Friedman then briefed Leslie Wexner, who concurred: "This is not Deborah's issue. It's much bigger than that." Then, with true visionary perspective, he said, "We could write a check to cover the costs, but this must be a communal effort. It can't be a Jew in Columbus helping a Jew in Atlanta fight the world's leading denier "

Wexner committed a significant sum but then rallied an entire team of people to solicit others. When I tried to thank Wexner a few weeks later, he impatiently brushed off my gratitude. "Forget the thanks. Our job is to ensure that you have the means to fight. Your job is to fight." The fight had been transformed beyond just being my own. It now belonged to the Jewish People.

Friedman next asked David Harris, executive director of the American Jewish Committee, to house a defense fund. The committee agreed and then made a major contribution to the fund. The Anti-Defamation League and the Simon Wiesenthal Center also contributed. In an unprecedented display of organizational restraint, none of these organizations publicized what they were doing. Within weeks other contributions arrived, as one person quietly called another. Some donations were substantial. Others were small. Most came from Jews. Some came from non-Jews.

As Irving was British and the case was being tried in British courts, Les insisted that British Jews step up to the plate. This they did, sometimes kicking and screaming, however; Irving would get so much publicity, they feared, that irrespective of the outcome, he would emerge victorious. They suggested I settle. Anthony asked wryly what they thought my bottom line should be: "One million Jews? Two million? One gas chamber? Two? Three?" And they came around.

A few months before the trial Irving offered to drop the case if I apologized to him and agreed to the pulping of the remaining copies of my book. Knowing, however, the reams of evidence we had amassed proving Irving's extensive lies and conscious of the support behind me, I quickly declined.

Our victory extended far beyond this case. A stellar team of historians amassed additional research that conclusively exposed deniers' manipulations, distortions, and fabrications—including details on the annihilation process hitherto unknown. As a result, outside of hard-core deniers themselves, claims about the nonexistence of the Nazi killing process are today universally ridiculed.

Looking back, we should all stand in awe of what is possible when many people are brought together in pursuit of what is right. Though today I am often praised for fighting this fight, I know full well that I could not have prevailed alone. While a gifted team of lawyers and historians played pivotal roles, they were able to do so only because of Les Wexner, Herb Friedman, David Harris, and many other Jewish communal leaders, some of them anonymous or barely known at all. Les was right to insist that others stand with him. In a frequently fractured Jewish community where people and organizations sometimes worry more about the credit they will receive than the outcome, this case was a counterpoint. It was an exemplar of leadership, cooperation, and keeping one's eyes on the prize, not the plaque.

Leadership for the New Era

The Challenge / The Opportunity

DR. JOHN RUSKAY

Dr. John Ruskay earned his BA from the University of Pittsburgh and his PhD in Political Science from Columbia University. He has served as education director of the 92nd Street Y (1980–1985), vice chancellor of the Jewish Theological Seminary (1985–1993), and executive vice president and CEO of UJA-Federation of New York (1999–2014). His visionary leadership has earned him honorary doctorates from Hebrew Union College–Jewish Institute of Religion, the Jewish Theological Seminary, Yeshiva University, and the Reconstructionist Rabbinical College. Dr. Ruskay speaks nationally and has authored numerous articles about the challenges and opportunities facing the American Jewish community. In May 2016, President Barack Obama appointed Dr. Ruskay to a two-year term as a member of the United States Commission for International Religious Freedom. He and his wife, Robin, have five children and eight grandchildren.

Clear vision, strategy, and execution. That's what's required to achieve change—always has. I believe it always will.

I still vividly recall that first meeting back in 1986. Rabbi Maurice Corson, the first president of The Wexner Foundation, had gathered a small group to hear Leslie Wexner share his core thinking: Everything I have observed (he began)—in business, in government, in philanthropy — leads me to believe that the decisive determinant of success or failure is leadership. Strong leadership enables good companies to become great. Weak leadership leads strong companies to disappointment. Ditto in government and the philanthropic sectors. He then added (quite modestly) his impression that Jewish communal leadership was failing. Whether the rabbinate, Federations, Hillels, Jewish Community Centers, or elsewhere, he insisted, a strong future would require strong leadership.

In time, the hallmark of The Wexner Foundation, its insistence on choosing and educating potential leaders, emerged. Thirty years later, "Wexnerites" are recognized as an elite professional cadre.

But, the communal challenge is different from what it was in 1986. The challenge at hand is to continue the Wexner model of selecting "the best and the brightest," but the context in which American Jewry finds itself has markedly changed. Let me explain.

Modern Jewish history is usually dated to the French Revolution. Napoleon swept through Europe and invited Jews to leave the ghettos and other self-segregated communities and become participants in the evolving, industrializing, modernizing West. While Jews had primarily lived in our own semi-autonomous communities, European Jewry had to now negotiate living in the emerging, more open, modernizing cultures of Europe. Reform Judaism, Conservative Judaism, and Zionism emerged as responses; each developed schools of thought offering their view on what was needed to sustain Judaism and support Jewish identity while embracing modernity. Waves of immigrants in the latter part of the nineteenth century brought these emerging intellectual frameworks to America, and each built movements that shaped twentieth-century American and world Jewry.

American Jews thrived in the twentieth century. While poverty persisted, over time most American Jews experienced increasing affluence, influence, and acceptance. During the twentieth century, American Jews could increasingly attend the best universities and attain employment in virtually every economic sector. However, as Brandeis University professor Jonathan Sarna documented, until the 1980s American cultural norms strongly favored in-marriage—among religious and ethnic groups—maintaining the Jewish community as a "kept community." The norm of in-marriage in America began to weaken in the 1960s, and by the 1980s, American Jewry found itself in the most accepting society where Jews had ever lived.

It ought be acknowledged, if parenthetically, that there were traditional segments of European Jewry who believed from the outset that modernity would inevitably erode Jewish commit-ment; that modern values emphasizing individualism and mate-rial acquisition were antithetical to Jewish values. Their heirs are among the thriving Haredi communities today in New York, Israel, and throughout the world. Their strength and birth rates seem to ensure a strong Jewish future.

Hence our question: how to sustain and strengthen Jewish life for those who seek to embrace modernity and Judaism? And for this challenge, we are thoroughly ill prepared. How could we be prepared? As members of a kept community, we had focused on the well-being of the millions of immigrants who reached our shores during the great migration (1881–1924); then focused on res-cuing three million Jews from the ashes of the Holocaust and build-ing the Jewish state; and later still, focused on rescuing Soviet Jews and airlifting Ethiopian Jews to Israel. These were the urgent chal-lenges that required the attention of American Jewry and its leader-ship, and the record of accomplishment in each was remarkable.

The present challenge is decidedly different. Can we create Jewish life that is sufficiently meaningful and compelling, that Jews will choose to self-identify as Jewish not because they have to— they do not; not because of guilt—they have little; but because of the meaning and purpose they experience in Jewish life? This is the challenge; this is the opportunity.

We now need to recruit and train leaders who understand their mandate as building inspired communities that can sear the soul and enable young and old to experience the inspiration and power of Jewish life. Institutions established as training grounds for a dif-ferent era will need to reconceptualize what will be required and to rebuild curricula accordingly. We need leaders who recognize the challenge and opportunity of forging communities of meaning and purpose.

We will need to acknowledge that we do not yet know how to do this nor are we clear on the leadership skills and profiles that will be required to undertake this new agenda. This work will not be accomplished in a year or even a decade. This will be the agenda for the next era of Jewish history.

There is erosion under way today, to be sure—continuing assimilation first and foremost. But there is also extraordinary renewal in Jewish life. The North American Jewish community is increasingly focusing on the internal fabric of our community and strengthening identity. JCCs and Ys seek new ways to connect and offer content. Forward-looking synagogues are embracing transformative models of prayer, study, and engagement. In just twelve years, five hundred thousand young men and women have participated in Birthright Israel, and Masa, the strongest Birthright follow-up to date, has tripled in but seven years. Hillels, Chabad, and a variety of Jewish study programs are reaching far more college students than ever before. Start-ups are emerging and Jewish social action groups are proliferating everywhere.

Demographic data remains troubling, to be sure, but we are in the first chapters of an entirely new era of Jewish history: living in the most open, accepting society which Jews have ever lived. Leadership will be decisive, as it has always been. For the leaders of tomorrow will determine whether Jewish communal life is compelling, engaging, and inspiring—or not. A prodigious challenge—and opportunity.

▲

Challenges in Israel

Leader as Gatekeeper

Battling Corruption in a Diverse Democracy

Avia Alef, Adv, LLM, MC-MPA

Avia Alef, Adv, LLM, MC-MPA, is an adjunct professor in the faculties of law at the Hebrew University of Jerusalem and Tel Aviv University. Until April 2013 she headed the Department of Economic Crimes in the State Attorney's Office at the Ministry of Justice. She has chaired (or been a member of) a variety of committees dealing with such subjects as the prohibition of money laundering and furthering the rights of children. She holds an LLB and an LLM from the Hebrew University and an MPA from Harvard's John F. Kennedy School of Government, as a Wexner Israel fellow.

Corruption in all its guises—political, corporate, or legal—is a contagious disease that is likely to run rampant if it is not countered by an aggressive and timely response that attacks it at its root. If left unchecked, it increases economic disparity and social inequality to the point of intimidating foreign investment and undermining the social and economic fabric altogether. Eventually, it pollutes the sense of public trust, eradicating the democratic foundations of society itself.

The comparison of public corruption in Israel to the rest of the world is not a pretty picture. Last year, the International Index of Corruption, which examines the level of corruption as perceived by experts, business leaders, and the public at large, placed Israel in 32nd place (out of 168 states) with a score of 61. Of the 32 states in the OECD (the Organization for Economic Cooperation and Development), Israel did even worse: it placed 24th, far behind Finland, Sweden, New Zealand, the United States, and Denmark (which was rated least corrupt, with a score of 91).

How do we explain Israel's high level of corruption? Every society has natural tendencies toward corruption—the temptation to exercise power for one's own benefit is universal—but Israel is, in addition, a vastly diverse society, built relatively rapidly (for just over half a century) by immigrants who arrive from all over the globe with little prior knowledge of democracy and bringing their own ideas of right and wrong. This dramatic demographic diversification occurred, moreover, partially simultaneously with economic instability.

The existence of so many diverse groups bringing ethical values from their home country (many of them not democratic) increases the propensity toward corruption, not out of a nakedly evil impulse to act illegally, but because of the lack of uniform moral norms that everyone accepts as properly binding on those with power to act otherwise. We need to ask how a diverse democracy like Israel can enforce a sense of national morality that overrides the diverse moral systems that various immigrant groups bring with them.

Such a national system would agree first on a definition of corruption as "abuse of power for personal profit, job, or private benefit." A related concept drawn from Jewish tradition itself would see the public servant as a *sh'liach tzibbur*, "an appointed agent of the public," which is to say, someone who should serve the public interest. Toward this end alone, he or she is entrusted with administrative or executive power, under the presumption that such power will be used for the exclusive good of the public, not one's self-interests.

There are various types of corruption: taking or giving bribes, using one's influence or authority for personal gain, exercising power inappropriately, and so on. Unfortunately, the Israeli public has seen all of that being done by our *sh'lichei tzibbur*. The Israeli legislature has itself passed a series of acts defining offenses that constitute corruption, including bribery, fraud, and breach of trust. Yet the problem remains.

No democratic society, especially one as free and diverse as ours, can afford to depend on the force of law alone as its only tool to battle corruption. It must also draw on such supplementary measures as education and ethics, and it must strengthen the role of the gatekeepers, the institutional guardians of propriety, beginning with the attorney general and the state comptroller, the whistle blowers who inform the general public of anything inappropriate or illegal. These are measures that prevent immoral actions from occurring one step before criminal charges.

Recently, politicians of the third largest party in Israel, Israel Beitenu, were investigated for allegations dealing with illegal money transfers into local government and various nonprofit organizations. It turned out that senior public officials were accepting bribes to appoint certain people to key positions. Why didn't alarm bells go off? The investigation revealed the routine practice of appointing gatekeepers from among the same party that they were supposed to watch over. These gatekeepers preferred to ignore the various illegalities rather than sound the alarms.

It is the role of leaders to take the high moral ground and ask difficult questions. Who are our government's gatekeepers? What stakeholders benefit from their turning a blind eye? What are the gatekeepers' ethical obligations? How can a diverse demographic society educate its multifaceted public to accept a national moral standard in place of the local standards that were imported from different cultures? How do we conceptualize the task of integrating the various elements of our diverse society into a strong democracy with a shared disdain for corruption? How do we create a united and uniform set of ethical values for everybody? In other words: how do we achieve fair and just forms of democratic life in conditions of significant demographic diversity, such as we have in Israel?

Three avenues of approach suggest themselves. We can learn from our history as the Jewish People, finding models in the biblical prophets, for example. Alternatively, trusting in the institution of professionalization—part and parcel of the Jewish People's entry into modernity—we can charge lawyers in general (and in public service, particularly) with overseeing and even playing the role of gatekeeper. And finally, we can expect that each of us takes a role, out of a sense of responsibility to society and the need to create a culture of accountability for the future.

▲▼▲▼▲▼▲▼▲▼▲▼▲▼▲

Speaking Up for Israel's Voiceless

Sharon Abraham-Weiss, Adv, LLM, MC-MPA

Sharon Abraham-Weiss, Adv, LLM, MC-MPA, was born in Israel's southernmost tip and is executive director of the Association for Civil Rights in Israel, Israel's oldest and largest human rights organization. In 2005, she was featured in *The Marker* as one of the top ten most influential people working for social change in Israel. In May 2014, *Haaretz* called her one of sixty-six prominent women leaders in Israel. She holds a BSc and an LLB from the Hebrew University, LLM from Tel-Aviv University, and MPA from Harvard's John F. Kennedy School of Government, where she was a Wexner fellow.

I head up the Association for Civil Rights in Israel (ACRI), the country's largest human-rights organization. Its storied history goes back more than four decades. Thanks to the dedicated people working at ACRI, some of the most important advances in civil liberties and human rights in Israel's history have been achieved. Working there has been both a dream come true and the biggest professional challenge of my life.

Our organization mirrors all the faces in Israel, a diversity that people in the West mistakenly overlook. Looking in on us from the outside, it is easy to imagine that everything happening here is somehow related to the conflict with our neighbors, a conflict that is deep, real, and sad. But at the same time (like all countries),

Israel has its haves and have-nots. Traditionally, the haves come from one background and the have-nots from another. I am from the other.

I was born in the South, in Eilat. The South is not just Eilat's glitzy hotels and sun-drenched beaches. It is also Israel's forgotten backyard. Those of us who grew up there were not expected to join the elite from the center of the country. I never wanted to believe the people who said that my very background disqualified me from prospering and making a difference. But they did tell me that; I had to fight that perception; and I know better than most that fighting for civil rights means fighting for the disadvantaged. ACRI is the voice of those who otherwise go unheard.

My grandparents were Holocaust survivors, a reality that etched two things into my mind from a very young age: first, that the Jewish People need a home, and second, that this Jewish national home must offer justice and fairness to all its inhabitants. One of the lessons of the Shoah is that atrocities happen when the voice of justice is silenced. I want to live in a society that sets an example of how minorities ought to be treated. My grandparents' story showed me what can happen in a society that fails to speak up for justice. Growing up as a minority in Israel myself only drove the message home.

Israel is a land of law, but also of contradictions. We affirm equality for all citizens, yet we elect governments that would chip away at that equality. We are proud of our culture that insists on "speaking our minds," yet we promulgate laws that would silence dissenting voices. We extol the idea that everyone is created *b'tzelem Elohim* (in the image of God), yet we marginalize anyone who falls outside the mainstream.

Two of ACRI's signal achievements illustrate this commitment: the Supreme Court decisions in the cases of Alice Miller and of Adel and Iman Kaadan.

Alice Miller was an immigrant from South Africa who came to Israel with a pilot's license in hand. When she joined the Israel Defense Forces in 1993, her application to enter the prestigious air force pilot training course was turned down because she was a woman. With ACRI's help, she petitioned the Supreme Court to compel the air force to admit her, and she won. The decision established gender equality as a fundamental principle of Israeli jurisprudence.

In another case, ACRI represented Adel and Iman Kaadan in their petition to be allowed to buy land in Katzir, a village near Umm El-Fahm in central Israel. Adel, a registered nurse, and Iman, a teacher, wanted to raise their children in a community that enjoys the same benefits and safety as are afforded to the small Jewish settlements in the region. Their request was denied out of hand on the grounds that the Kaadans are Arabs, while the land on which the village is built was leased from the Jewish National Fund and intended exclusively for Jews. ACRI's lawyers argued that denying the couple's request on the grounds of their ethnicity amounts to illegal discrimination. In a 4 to 1 vote, the court agreed. In a way, this case was Israel's *Brown v. Board of Education* (the 1954 U.S. Supreme Court decision that made racial segregation in schools illegal).

I have chosen a path that involves me in defending the fairness, equality, and personal liberties guaranteed in Israel's Declaration of Independence. I oppose the current Israeli lawmakers who betray that democratic character. I do this with the confidence that, as Martin Luther King Jr. said, "The arc of the moral universe is long, but it bends towards justice." I do this because equality is not only a universal right but also a hallowed Jewish value.

It was as a Wexner fellow that I was formed to do this work. I was introduced to an amazingly diverse group of people, whose views have shaped my own and enriched my horizons. I have thrown in my lot with today's generation of Jewish leaders who understand that injustice anywhere is injustice everywhere, and protecting our Jewish character in Israel means first and foremost protecting our democracy.

▲ ▲▼▲ ▲▼▲ ▲▼▲ ▲▼▲ ▲

Stop Feeling Sorry for Disabled Children

(Start Respecting Them Instead)

Dr. Maurit Beeri

Dr. Maurit Beeri graduated from medical school and trained as a pediatrician at Hebrew University Hadassah Medical Center in Jerusalem. She holds an MPA from Harvard's John F. Kennedy School of Government, as a Wexner Israel fellow. Concerned especially with promoting cultural competency in health, she led ALYN Jerusalem to become the first culturally competent hospital in Israel. She is now the director general of ALYN Hospital Pediatric and Adolescent Rehabilitation Center and director of its Multidisciplinary Clinic for Infants and Children with Feeding Disorders. She is especially active in promoting the rights of children with special needs. Dr. Beeri and her husband, Professor Ronen Beeri, are parents of three boys and caretakers to two cats.

Several weeks ago, I overheard a conversation between two kids, Or and Esther, from our rehabilitation preschool day-care center. Or announced confidently that he intends on taking Esther to be his wife. Esther, far from impressed, retorted, "I'll *never* marry you! You don't observe Shabbat!"

At that moment my heart went out to the disheartened-looking boy. But at the same time, I felt a sense of gratitude for this witty conversation and the mutual understanding between the two preschoolers. Although Esther is paralyzed from her neck down and both children are dependent on a respiration machine, their disabilities played no role in the exchange—their physical condition remained in the background, just another fact of life.

Looking at Esther and Or, I realized that their parents, teachers, caregivers, and society at large are tasked with the responsibility to create a society and culture in which it is not their disability that dictates their future, but their personal values, just like the rest of us.

Leadership, I have learned, is far more than just being in the lead. It is effecting change. The change for which I strive is to get society to stop feeling sorry for children with disabilities and start respecting them instead.

Seven years in medical school, a five-and-a-half-year residency in pediatrics, and fifteen years in the field of child rehabilitation have taught me that most people—even the kindest of them—are gravely misinformed when it comes to children with disabilities. Contrary to popular opinion, impairment and disability are not purely physical; rather, they are predominantly a reflection of the subjective and an indefinable gap between our expectations of ourselves and what we really are. Children who are raised with pity grow up viewing themselves as pitiable and, as such, lead pitiful lives. Individuals pitied as children have a greater likelihood of becoming needy adults, unable to hold themselves to a high standard of achievement.

If we wish to raise well-adjusted children with the life skills they will need as adults, we must stop feeling sorry for them and learn instead to treat them as we would any other child.

Disability is just one single aspect of the larger whole we call growing up. Warmth, love, clear boundaries, encouragement to explore and enjoy life—all these are even more important for children with disabilities than for their peers who are "typically developed" (as children without disabilities are referred to).

In an age when modern medicine and technology are advancing at breakneck speed, the gap between being disabled and fully functional no longer depends entirely on physical ability. Each year, new technologies allow disabled people to function at a level that may even catch up with their non-disabled peers and, perhaps, even exceed them. I do not mean just eyeglasses, hearing aids, and wheelchairs; today's medical achievements reach far beyond this sort of thing. Gastric feeding devices and mobile respirators, for example, allow many disabled people to enjoy a fully functional life in the comfort of their own homes and beyond.

Society as a whole is increasingly dependent on technology that allows us to function beyond our natural abilities. We cover great distances on land and in the air, we communicate digitally, and we extend the capacity of our brains by using huge memory storage devices as if they were a trivial feat. These same developments, however, shorten the gap between the typically developed and the disabled, both of whom can use the new technologies with equal capacity. Does it make any difference whether this essay was typed using a QWERTY keyboard or an eye-tracking device used by people who cannot use their fingers? The main point is that I can clearly say what I want to.

To be sure, physical disabilities remain challenges—I do not mean to paper over the way that people in wheelchairs, say, must make adjustments that walkers never worry about. Nor do I claim that life is just as easy or that the world of opportunity is just as available to those who are homebound and those who are not. But the real disability is not so much the physical challenges as it is the way society treats those who face them. At stake is the way we inhibit individuals from becoming active members of society, by perpetuating their role as objects of misery and inadequacy and making them feel needy to the point of being devoid of a sense of purpose.

Children with disabilities do need special help growing up; they do require special support to become well-adjusted adults and equal members of society. But raised merely on sympathy, pity, and charity rather than love, respect, and encouragement is an injustice that sidelines them from society's mainstream.

Hillel said famously, "If I am not for myself, who will be for me? If I am only for myself, what am I? And if not now, when?"[1] These are precisely the three goals of "rehabilitation" for the disabled: to enable them "to be for themselves"—to manage life's daily routine independently; to develop their self-identity in a way that allows them "to be not just for themselves" — to give to others, not just to take; and to foster their own sense of urgency, a belief that they can become capable "now," for "if not now, when?"

Toward these ends, the disabled need better resources, proper laws and regulations, bigger budgets, and more flexibility in the social system upon which we all depend. Their ease of access must extend beyond such obvious aids as wheelchair ramps, braille, and audio signals. A fully supportive environment is imperative if little Or and Esther are to get a chance to become adults filled with self-respect rather than self-pity.

Once society treats the disabled as we treat their non-disabled peers, providing equal privileges and equal obligations, as full partners with those around them, we can hope to see them as tomorrow's respected and equal members of society.

▲ ▲▼▲ ▲▼▲ ▲▼▲ ▲▼▲ ▲

Out of the Shtetl

A Mature, Confident, and Constructive Zionism

Nadav Tamir

Nadav Tamir was born and raised on Kibbutz Manara in northern Israel, served in the IDF (retiring with the rank of major), and graduated magna cum laude with a BA in philosophy and political science from the Hebrew University of Jerusalem. He has served as consul general of Israel to New England, political officer at the Israeli Embassy in Washington, DC, and a member of the Israeli Ministry of Foreign Affairs under three foreign ministers: Shimon Peres, Ehud Barak, and David Levy. He became senior policy adviser to President Perez and now directs international policy and government affairs at Peres & Associates Global Advisory LTD. As a Wexner Israel fellow, he earned his MPA from Harvard's John F. Kennedy School of Government. He has authored articles in both scholarly and popular modes and now chairs the Wexner-Israel Alumni Association. He is the father of Maya, Ido, and Naama.

The State of Israel today faces an unprecedented "adaptive challenge." I borrow the term from Ronald Heifetz, who differentiates technical challenges (where a straightforward answer is known, at least to somebody) from adaptive challenges that demand a new approach, including considerable negotiated conversation, just to diagnose the issue, let alone solve it.[1]

The Adaptive Challenge

Zionism sought to normalize the Jewish People by transforming it from a victim of history into an entity with control over its own destiny. This normalization has brought about enormous Israeli successes, primarily in the private sector, which has emphasized values like entrepreneurship, dynamism, and risk-taking. These flow from confidence in our capabilities in science, economics, and the arts, to the point where Israel is widely considered a model of creativity and innovation.

By contrast, the official State of Israel—the political echelon and the public sector—demonstrates the opposite. Israel's foreign policy and approach to national security are characterized by a sense of insecurity that engenders defensiveness and reaction—just the opposite of creativity.

How do we explain this gap between the "start-up nation"[2]—the country that turns every crisis into an opportunity, initiating, taking risks, creating world-enhancing ideas—and the political Israel that sees every development through the prism of the "worst-case scenario"? How do we explain the gap between the international community's perception of Israel as strong and secure and our perception of ourselves as weaklings?

During a visit to concentration camps in Poland, it hit me: *we are a traumatized nation*. Discussions of security and foreign affairs evoke the primal fear that once again, "they are out to destroy us. You can't trust the *goyim*. They're all anti-Semites." Put another way, we might say that we successfully removed the Jew from the shtetl but have yet to remove the shtetl from the Jew.

Paralyzed by shtetl-like fear, we allow politicians to revert to defensive inaction and the redundant recourse to old solutions that regularly turn out wrong. Only an adaptive approach will convert our "victim-like" foreign policy into a path-breaking and successful one.

Self-Confidence and Constructive Optimism

We cannot ignore genuine threats, but we need a more balanced vision of reality. Optimism does not just describe reality, it impacts it; cautious optimism creates opportunities, not just obstacles. By contrast, a negative perspective creates negative "self-fulfilling prophecies." When we say, "The whole world is against us," we cause the world to be against us. When we say, "There is no partner for peace," we behave in a way that guarantees we have no partner.

Modern Israel's founders, who created "something out of nothing" (*yesh mei'ayin*), against all odds, chose "Hope" (*Hatikvah*) as the name of our national anthem. Somewhere along the way, we have lost faith in hope and in its enabling powers. In order to re-create the hopeful state of mind that our founders once had, we need what Marshall Ganz calls "a hopeful heart and a critical eye."[3]

Beyond Winning

It is no coincidence that in Hebrew, the term "zero-sum game" is translatable, but "win-win" is not! Our victim-like approach sees only winners and losers and promotes winning at all costs. We prefer to win the debate, while what we really need to win is hearts and minds.

At a workshop on negotiation that I attended at Harvard Law School, we were divided into couples for a game of arm wrestling and told that for each time we had the upper hand we'd get ten dollars. Most of the participants wrestled with each other; only a few realized they would gain more by cooperating.

Our conventional approach sees empathy and assertiveness as mutually exclusive, whereas, in truth, empathy promotes the interests of both sides, including our own, letting both sides win.[4] Looking for shared interests rather than victory would permit our political establishment to forgo military action when solutions can be better achieved through what Joseph S. Nye Jr. calls "soft power."[5] We have created a sophisticated and effective army but too often revert to force when diplomatic measures might be more effective.

Accountability and Openness to Criticism

A victim-like approach fosters "the blame game"—seeing a traitor in anyone who expresses the need for our own constructive self-criticism. Instead of altering the substance of what we are, we depend on *hasbarah*—justifying and explaining away our troublesome stances. Yet research demonstrates that people do not change their worldviews because of the other side's logical explanations.[6]

A Forward-Looking Approach

Under normal circumstances, the human mind grasps the linear flow of time and extrapolates from former changes to expected future ones. In a world where change occurs exponentially, however, that approach is problematic,[7] especially for traumatized people too stuck in the past to imagine a new future altogether. Military, government, and research institutes are therefore coming to see that rather than trying to predict the future as they used to, they need to map alternative scenarios alongside the capacity for rapid adaptation, learning, and flexibility.[8]

Most of us are still "stuck" with anachronistic notions born of old paradigms. But the paradigm has changed, leaving a gap between reality and our perception of it.[9] I participated in discussions on change in the Middle East after the riots in Tahrir Square, where it was clear that those who found it most difficult to grasp the changes were the experts! They were the ones who were mired in an irrelevant paradigm.

Summary

Dealing with our adaptive challenge requires leadership transformed into operating out of hope, not fear; inspiration, not desperation. We must seek win-win situations and embrace reflection and self-criticism. Paradigms of a past are no longer workable.

We may yet fulfill the Zionist dream to transform the Jewish People from a victim of history to a contributing force in our region and the world. By taking the initiative in foreign relations we can establish an Israel that is not only secure and prosperous, but aligned with the international community and with its neighbors—attractive to its own citizens and to the Jewish People at large.

▲ ▲▼▲ ▲▼▲ ▲▼▲ ▲▼▲ ▲

Gender in the IDF

Promoting Women Leadership in a Male Organization

BRIGADIER GENERAL RACHEL TEVET WIESEL

Brigadier General Rachel Tevet Wiesel received her LLB and LLM degrees from Bar Ilan University. She has served as a chief justice of the IDF Central Command, Home Front Command and General Staff Units, and Israeli Air Force (IAF) Military Tribunal and as head of Alesha's Supervision Branch. She is now adviser to the Chief of the General Staff on Gender Issues of the Israeli Defense Forces (IDF).

> "The highest degree of equality is the equality of duties, and the highest level of duty is that of defense … and as long as women are not equal to men in performing this duty, there can be no full and real equality."
>
> —DAVID BEN-GURION (1948)

Thanks to the Security Service Law that established compulsory service for men and women alike as far back as 1949, women have been integral to the IDF (Israeli Defense Force) since its inception. David Ben-Gurion intended it as no mere theoretical concept, but instead an actual goal: the call to integrate thousands of women into the war efforts of the new state—women who, frequently, had fought alongside the British against the Nazis and in the pre-state

Jewish underground that opposed the British Mandate prior to Israel's founding.

Egalitarian integration of women in the military is important not only for the IDF, which benefits from their significant contribution (more than 30 percent of the IDF workforce are women). It is also essential for Israeli society as a whole, since the IDF, "the People's Army," is a major social mechanism for the civic, moral, and professional formation of Israel's citizens. In many cases, military service becomes an instrument of social mobility for new immigrants and diverse social classes, who acquire skills that can be converted into social and economic capital once they return to civilian life. It would not be too much to say that *the IDF is the most important social arena for achieving substantive gender equality of opportunity*.

Fortunately, the IDF is indeed committed to substantive equality between the sexes, but there are significant built-in barriers to success. The IDF is, after all (by definition), a combat organization with a perceived overlap between combat and masculinity, so that many roles and positions are reserved solely for men. In addition (although much progress has been made), the army was created by and for men, so that many of its operating ideas, processes, and practices are still geared to the needs and traits of men, not women.

The organizational challenge facing the IDF is to accommodate both male and female leadership models as equally legitimate entities, side by side. To achieve this important goal, women in the IDF generally, and I particularly—as the advisor on gender to the chief of staff—face the challenge of initiating and developing the process by which current perceptions, processes, and practices can be exchanged for egalitarian alternatives—without, of course, detracting from the effectiveness of the organization.

So, how do we do it? With three approaches, some already largely implemented, others less so.

First, by promoting legal and formal measures that bear on issues of gender equality, like opening most of the military professions for both men and women, equalizing duration of service in most IDF-related professions, and fully applying such existing regulations as a six-month maternity leave and, even, paternity leave for men—not to mention, full enforcement of the law preventing sexual harassment. These (and other examples) will also require regularized updating of commands and procedures in the IDF as time moves on.

Second, by confronting structural and infrastructural obstacles that create inequality: unifying officers' courses for men and women; holding co-ed training sessions for all positions that are open to both women and men; dealing with career tracks that are suitable for mothers (and fathers); combining field and headquarters activities; providing replacements for mothers on maternity leave, so that integrating pregnant women will no longer be an obstacle; and procuring and supplying suitable equipment for women so they can perform a larger number of roles.

Third, by altering masculine perceptions that are the backbone of IDF organization and operations. At stake will be changing the entire corporate culture, where desirable, and shattering conventions, where possible. More specifically, the IDF will have to change the prevalent images regarding the ideal senior commander as male and enhance gender awareness by helping men and women assimilate appropriate gender concerns in every decision-making process in which they are involved (*gender mainstreaming*).

No single one of these strategies is sufficient. We need all three—as the kids say, "This, that, and that as well."

The IDF has come a long way since its founding under Ben-Gurion. It should be proud of the way it has progressed from the initial vision of integrating women into the army of the new state (albeit mainly in traditional roles) to today's integration of women into combat units (two co-ed combat battalions were opened just last year). Women also serve now in areas of advanced technology, cyber, medicine, intelligence, field training, pilots' and naval officers' courses, and more.

This progress derives not just from changing external conditions (like the need for personnel), but also from the initiative and leadership of women and men who believe that a gender-equal IDF is a stronger and better army from both the organizational and the operational perspectives.

In sum, we are challenged today to help the IDF establish feminine leadership models through which women alongside men may advance in the military, joining hands to grapple effectively with the challenges of the coming years. This is an important step toward enhancing the strength and power of the IDF itself; but also (no less importantly), it will enhance the health and well-being of Israeli society in its entirety.

The Enduring Leadership of David Ben-Gurion, Israel's Eternal "Old Man"

Major General (retired) Amos Yadlin

Major General (retired) Amos Yadlin is the executive director of the Institute for National Security Studies (INSS) in Israel. From 2006 to 2010, he served as Israel's chief of defense intelligence. Prior to that, he served as the IDF attaché to the United States. In February 2002, he earned the rank of major general and was named commander of the IDF Military Colleges and the National Defense College. Over the course of his career, he accumulated about five thousand flight hours, flew more than two hundred combat missions behind enemy lines, and participated in the Yom Kippur War (1973), Operation Peace for Galilee (1982), and Operation Tamuz—the destruction of the Osirak nuclear reactor in Iraq (1981). He holds a BA with honors in economics and business administration from Ben-Gurion University of the Negev and an MPA from Harvard's John F. Kennedy School of Government.

David Ben-Gurion, known admiringly in Israel as "the Old Man," passed away over forty years ago, but his leadership continues to resonate. Even today, his unique blend of integrity and strength serves as a compass for Israeli society, which yearns for a leader of similar stature and scale. Ben-Gurion remains the greatest modern Jewish leader. We all stand to learn from his example.

Ben-Gurion was both a pragmatist and an ideologue. He upheld a revolutionary vision and made it a reality through bold and realistic perseverance. In times of need, he would prioritize making strategic capitulations when necessary, but drawing lines in the sand when appropriate. He understood the importance of international support, for example, but when that support was conditioned on placing Israel's vital interests at risk, he fearlessly stood his ground. He preached peace but made it clear that war might be right around the corner. In international relations, he understood the preeminence of power, but he was unwilling to sacrifice morality while putting that power to use. In today's terms, Ben-Gurion was neither "right-wing" nor "left-wing." Rather, he remains, first and foremost, an exemplary model of Israeli statesmanship (*mamlachtiut*). Five cases, in particular, demonstrate this specific strength of his.

The Decision to Accept the UN's Plan for Partition

The year 1947 was a grim one for the Jewish People. The horrendous scale of the Holocaust was becoming apparent, and Arab violence was surging in the Land of Israel. With the November 29 United Nations' vote on Israeli-Arab partition, the leadership in Tel Aviv realized that a decisive moment was at hand.

The borders mandated by the UN partition plan were not viable and did not include Jerusalem. Accepting them was extremely difficult to stomach, but Ben-Gurion realized that at that particular moment in time, it was the best option he had. The horrors of the last decade demonstrated the necessity of having a safe refuge for Jews, and for years after the war's end, survivors of the Holocaust remained stranded in Europe due to British Mandatory authorities' refusal to grant them permission to immigrate to the Yishuv. Partition offered at least the possibility of establishing a sovereign Jewish state.

Gifted with the unique ability to think in historic-strategic terms, Ben-Gurion saw the 1947 borders as a sufficient starting point with potential to change for the better in the future.

Leadership is the ability to act within the constraints of realistic political options to achieve the primary moral goal, rather than to pursue unrealistic ambitions and risk ending up empty-handed.

The Decision to Declare the State of Israel

As Ben-Gurion predicted, the UN vote was followed by an increase in violence. With British forces on their way out, the Yishuv's leadership had to make another bold decision—whether to risk declaring a Jewish state, despite warnings from sympathizers, both at home and abroad, that such a precipitous announcement would prompt an immediate Arab invasion and a second Holocaust. The divided leadership turned to Ben-Gurion, who understood that the window of opportunity created by the UN vote of recognition might not last for long. He decided, therefore, to declare independence but also prepare for the possibility of war. While Israelis danced in the streets, Ben-Gurion summoned his General Staff and gave them orders of battle.

Leadership is the ability to recognize and seize a historic moment of opportunity that may never return in order to advance critical interests.

Ensuring Only One Military

Throughout the battles of 1948, Ben-Gurion was constantly challenged by rival pre-statehood underground forces like Etzel (the right-wing militia of Zionist Revisionists influenced by Ze'ev Jabotinski) and Lechi (a breakaway militia from Etzel established by Avraham Yair Stern). Among the difficult decisions that Ben-Gurion had to make to assure the unity of command and of governance was the sinking of the *Altalena*, a ship delivering weapons to Etzel. He similarly integrated the much lauded, but semi-independent Palmach brigades into the Israeli Defense Force (IDF). These decisions raised great controversy within the Israeli leadership and left marks on Israeli society that would take decades to heal. But Ben-Gurion's resolute decision ensured the existence of a single fighting force, the IDF, which reports to, and only to, the democratically elected Israeli government.

Leadership is fearless confrontation of contemporary currents or trends that threaten long-term stability, even at the cost of short-term conflict.

Forgoing Judea and Samaria

Toward the end of the War of Independence, Ben-Gurion faced another strategic choice: whether to order the IDF to seize as much land as possible or to stop at what would later be called the "Green Line." By late 1949, the IDF had momentum on all fronts and, from a purely military standpoint, could have seized control of the entire West Bank.

Ben-Gurion had a deep appreciation for the historic importance of the land in its entirety as the birthplace of the Jewish People, but he also understood the perils of "over-reaching," a situation in which more could very well mean less: the international community would have pressured the fledgling Israeli state to return to the far worse UN partition lines, and no less importantly, taking over those lands would instantly make Jews a minority in Israel. He understood perfectly the necessity for Israel to be Jewish without sacrificing its liberal democratic values.

Leadership is refusing to sacrifice basic moral values in pursuit of military or political success.

Insisting on Jerusalem

In late 1949, a UN General Assembly was convened. Unexpectedly, the Australian delegation proposed the internationalization of Jerusalem. Ben-Gurion countered by announcing the immediate transfer of all of Israel's government bureaus and even the Knesset itself to Jerusalem. To his senior ministers calling for a more gradual, subtle policy, Ben-Gurion declared Jerusalem to be "a vital Jewish interest—the heart of Israel." Against all grim predictions, the sky did not fall, and the world gradually grew to accept Jerusalem's centrality to Israel.

Leadership is taking the bold steps necessary to protect the core components of one's vital interests.

Ben-Gurion's Two Pillars

The leadership of Ben-Gurion is manifest in every corner of the modern Israeli state. While today's challenges differ radically from those of the past, Ben-Gurion's fundamental principles are still relevant. "The fate of Israel depends on its might and the justness of its cause," Ben-Gurion once said. If we are wise enough to uphold those two pillars in our national decision-making, we will achieve success worthy of the "old man."

▲

Challenges in America

American Jews Speak a "Jewish Language"

DR. SARAH BUNIN BENOR

Dr. Sarah Bunin Benor is associate professor of contemporary Jewish studies at Hebrew Union College–Jewish Institute of Religion. She received a PhD in linguistics from Stanford University in 2004 and has authored many articles and a book, *Becoming Frum: How Newcomers Learn the Language and Culture of Orthodox Judaism*. Dr. Benor's fellowships and prizes include the Dorot Fellowship in Israel, the Wexner Graduate Fellowship, and the Sami Rohr Choice Award for Jewish Literature. She is founding co-editor of the *Journal of Jewish Languages* and creator of the Jewish Language Research Website and the Jewish English Lexicon. She lives in Los Angeles with her husband, Mark, and their daughters, Aliza, Dalia, and Ariella.

Why should Jewish leaders think about language? Because it is a crucial part of communal cohesiveness. Humans use language not just to make a point but to identify who we are and to connect with our conversation partners. In the case of American Jews, we use "Jewish English" — English with Hebrew and Yiddish words and other distinctive features — to identify ourselves not just as Jews but as certain types of Jews: Reform, Hasidish, Talmudically trained, Israel-oriented, Persian, and so on.

Here are two examples of textually engaged Jewish English from e-mails sent to the Wexner Graduate Fellowship list:

- From a Modern Orthodox rabbi:

  Chevre [friends],
      I'm preparing a *shiur* [lesson] and could use a *mekor* [source]
  or two....
      Any *mefarshim* [commentators] on the *Avot* [forefathers]
  you might recommend? Any good *Chazals* [(teachings from)
  our sages, may their memories be blessed]? Where again is
  the *Gemarrah* [Talmud] on changing one's name in a time of
  teshuva [repentance]?...
      Any *mekorot* [sources] would be a real *chesed* [act of kind-
  ness] to me for my work.

- From a Reform rabbi:

  L'shem chinuch [for the sake of education], I am leading a
  "mock" *seder* [Passover ceremony] tomorrow for our Basic
  Judaism class.... I am wondering if anyone out there has
  already created ... an "essence of" *Haggadah* [seder booklet]
  that is more explanatory than *halachic* [according to Jewish
  law].... Thanks in advance for anything you might send my way.
  I'll teach it all *b'shem omro/omrah* [in the name of its speaker]!

These excerpts continue a millennia-long tradition of Diaspora
"Jewish languages,"[1] starting with Judeo-Aramaic and Judeo-
Greek and continuing with Judeo-Arabic, Judeo-Italian, Yiddish,
Ladino, and so on. I applaud this continuity. I disagree with cultural critic Leon Wieseltier's oft-cited claim, "The American Jewish
community is the first great community in the history of our people
that believes that it can receive, develop, and perpetuate the Jewish
tradition *not* in a Jewish language."[2] Clearly he is thinking about
Yiddish and Ladino as exemplars of Jewish linguistic history. But
most Diaspora Jewish communities actually spoke variants of the
local language, entities that we refer to as "Jewish languages."

   Like Judeo-Arabic, Judeo-Persian, and so on, Jewish English is
based on the local non-Jewish language (English) but with words
from Hebrew as well as other ancestral tongues (e.g., Yiddish,
Ladino, Arabic, Farsi). It also uses distinctive grammatical features ("Staying by us," "I don't know from calculus"), distinctive

pronunciations (Jews are more likely than non-Jews to pronounce the "o" in "Florida" and "horrible" with the New York "a," even when they're not from New York), and distinctive intonation patterns, especially among Orthodox Jews.

You're probably thinking: Minor differences like that don't make for a separate language. Isn't it just a dialect, if that?

One way of answering that question is to say that if speakers can understand each other, they speak *dialects* of the same language; if not, they speak different *languages*. Are the quotes above intelligible to Americans generally? Probably not; they might get the gist but miss much of the nuance. In that sense, it is a different language.

But the question of whether Jewish English (or Judeo-Berber, Judeo-Malayalam, and so forth) is a dialect or a language is unproductive. Instead, we should look at Diaspora Jewish communities as existing along a continuum of distinctness from the local language: some speak very similarly to their non-Jewish neighbors, and some speak very differently. Where do American Jews fall along this continuum? All over it, depending on who's speaking and to whom they're speaking. The same can be said for many Diaspora communities throughout history.

The debate about Jewish English should be of interest to anyone in leadership, not just scholars, because it touches on how contemporary Jews see themselves in relation to their ancestors and their religious tradition. Many agree with Wieseltier that American Jewishness is a radical break from the past, when Jews used, say, Yiddish when talking to one another, as opposed to Polish or Russian when talking to non-Jews. But when we look beyond Yiddish and Ladino to the fascinating history of Diaspora Jewish languages, we see that speaking English with Hebrew words and other distinctive features connects us not only with other American Jews but also with Jewish communities around the world over the last two millennia.

When I e-mailed the people whose quotes I used at the beginning of this article, they expressed concern that their use of so many Hebrew words makes them sound "silly" or "obnoxious."

And they're not alone. I regularly hear Jewish professionals and volunteers criticizing the mixing of Hebrew and English as incorrect or inappropriate. I disagree. These quotes exemplify the long-standing Diaspora practice of enhancing local language with words and phrases from our cultural heritage: our sacred texts and other ancestral languages (enriched now with Israeli Hebrew also).

I say it is time to embrace our linguistic distinctiveness. Let Jewish leaders proudly use Jewish English in speech and writing, translating Hebrew words for newcomers. Let Jewish educators socialize our youth to use Hebrew words within English sentences, in community-appropriate ways. And let us teach the history of Jewish languages, emphasizing Americans' place in that history. As we shift from language to language, may we go from strength to strength—*mechayil el chayil.*

The Tones of Leadership

Dr. David Bryfman

Dr. David Bryfman is currently the chief innovation officer at The Jewish Education Project in New York. He completed his PhD at New York University in education and Jewish studies and is an alumnus of Wexner Graduate Fellowship, class 17. After many years working in formal and informal Jewish education in Australia, Israel, and North America, he now lives in Brooklyn with his wife, Mirm, and two children, Jonah and Abby.

Nachamu nachamu ami: "Comfort, comfort My people, says your God" (Isaiah 40:1). I first read these words as my bar mitzvah portion, thirty years ago. If it isn't actual destiny, it is at least ironic that all these years later, I see in them a core leadership struggle of our time.

I have little doubt that when given a choice most people prefer leaders who deliver inspiration, encouragement, and consolation rather than chastisement, criticism, and rebuke. But which of the two is more likely to produce the changes that we need?

My office sports a poster that reads, "Innovate or Die!"—the title also of a presentation that I gave to Jewish communal professionals, educators, and clergy. The session didn't go so well, to say the least. From the opening slide that featured this slogan the audience was on the defensive. Apparently they didn't like the choice

I was offering; maybe both of my options—innovate or die—were too threatening.

I thought back to Nietzsche's observation that people "refuse to accept an idea merely because the tone of voice in which it has been expressed is unsympathetic." One month later I delivered exactly the same presentation to a very similar audience, but I changed the title from "Innovate or Die" to "The Innovation Imperative." This time the presentation was widely praised, the excitement in the room was palpable, and some people even called the session transformative.

What is clear here is the lesson that words matter. With "die" in the title, people became defensive. When "die" became "imperative," they felt a call to action. More substantive still is the difference between a message framed in doom and gloom and one that embodies aspiration. The cliché rings true: it's often not what you say, but how you say it that really counts. In the words of poet Maya Angelou (a person who knows how to say it), "People don't always remember what you say or even what you do, but they always remember how you made them feel."

Yet I remain haunted by a gnawing recognition that this world needs leaders who do not acquiesce to telling people what they want to hear. The kinder, gentler approach, often associated with compassionate leaders, may motivate a population to tweak or adjust their behavior. But will it produce the wholesale change or radical transformation that might be necessary? Perhaps it takes the critical, tell-it-like-it-is approach to awaken people from their slumber and bring about the large disruptive changes that we sometimes need. Isn't that what leadership is all about?

The Jewish community today prefers leadership that's warm and comforting, which isn't terribly surprising. After all, who would voluntarily subject themselves to a rabbi's sermon that made them feel like crap? Why would someone belong to an organization whose refrain was "Our work is never done"? Why would someone attend a lecture or a performance that had them leaving in a state of despair? The truth is that when given a choice, most people choose ease over tension or discomfort. And maybe that is why our Jewish community stagnates with inability to adapt to the realities of the world in which we live.

I work at the intersection of education and innovation, continually facing the question, How can we make Jewish learning and engagement relevant to the young people and families of today? So much has changed in the decades since our institutions of Jewish learning were first established! Surely mechanisms for doing what they do—and the educators who actually do it—must adapt accordingly.

I can suggest to you, gently, that you might want to consider changing the way you run your school/camp/youth group if you want to become more engaging. Or, I can tell you outright that if you don't dramatically change the way you operate, young Jews will continue walking away, you'll soon be out of business, and because of your failure, the next generation will be lost to Judaism forever. Which message would you *prefer* to hear? Which one do you *need* to hear?

Several factors may influence the tone that leaders adopt in delivering their messages. Stereotypes aside, considerable literature differentiates the comforting feminine approach to leadership from a more aggressive masculine leadership posture.[1] Other research highlights cultural differences—it is less socially acceptable to rebuke someone in the workplace of the United States, for example, than in Israel, Russia, or Germany.[2] As a Jewish Australian living in the United States, I regularly note how leadership personas reflect those social and cultural norms in which we find ourselves embedded.

With many good dichotomies, the answer lies somewhere in between, so maybe we should conclude that leaders ought to fill their arsenals with both comfort and rebuke (*n'chemta* and *toch'chah*) and choose between them as circumstances require. But there are a lot of comforting voices at play, a lot of telling people what they want to hear, in a way that they want to hear it—and maybe, just maybe, what we need right now is a bit more toughness from our leaders—the tough love that makes a difference.

Afterword

The original draft of this piece had a very different tone and outcome. This started as a piece about my own learning over time about the importance of adding a more comforting persona to my leadership style. But a few important developments occurred in the last few months, including a conversation with my mother, in the last few days of her life, that shined refreshing light on the necessity of occasionally taking a more critical—a "no bullshit"— approach when you want to see change occur. This article is dedicated to my mother, Sonia Bryfman *z"l* (1946–2015), who passed away as I was writing it, and who had a reputation of always telling it like it was—with love and with refreshing candor.

Orthodox Jewish Feminism on the Rise

Offense Is Your Best Defense

DR. SHARON WEISS-GREENBERG

Dr. Sharon Weiss-Greenberg, now executive director of the Jewish Orthodox Feminist Alliance (JOFA), has a BA in sociology and Jewish history and a master's degree in education from Yeshiva University, and a PhD from New York University. She is an alumna of the Wexner Graduate Fellowship/Davidson Scholar Program and was named by the *Jewish Week* as a person to watch, one of their "36 Under 36" honorees. She has taught at Yeshiva University High School for Girls in New York, Yavneh Academy in New Jersey, and the Denver Academy of Torah High School. She served also as the co-director and Orthodox adviser of the Orthodox Union Jewish Learning on Campus Initiative at Harvard Hillel, as the first Orthodox woman chaplain at Harvard University, and as the *rosh moshava* (head of) Camp Stone.

There is a unique clarity that players experience on the basketball court. Take the simple feeling of bouncing that ball on the shiny hardwood flooring on your way down the court. The noise is deafening: spectators cheering, chattering, eating, and milling about; opponents yelling instructions as they calculate defensive strategy. But while dribbling that ball, your mind remains clear:

you block out the noise, chart the movement of teammates, focus on passing or shooting or whatever it takes to set up a winning play. It's a Zen-like experience.

Defense is different: instead of planning a play, you are responding to one. If they shift left, you shift left; if they shift right, you shift right. Instead of scoring points to move forward, you fight to keep things the same. You run, sweat, and jump just to keep the status quo.

Being an Orthodox feminist is like playing basketball—you hear noise all around you. But it is far more complex, because critics come not just from the other team but from everyone—on the left and on the right and even from within. So very many people want you to lose the game, to just pack your bag and go home.

Historically, Judaism and feminism have not been strangers. Judith Kaplan celebrated her bat mitzvah in 1922. The Reform movement ordained its first woman, Sally Priesand, in 1972; the Conservative movement followed suit with Amy Eilberg in 1985. Yet the Orthodox rabbinate continues to reject the advancement of women as disingenuous and wrong.

But change is in the air. In 2006, while teaching at Yeshiva University High School for Girls, I discussed the different Jewish denominations and spoke about the closest thing to women in the rabbinate that existed in Orthodoxy, Nishmat's Yoatzot Halacha, where women study to become experts in the laws of family purity. A student with extremely conservative views regarding politics and religion surprised me by asking, "If a woman can advise on *niddah* [laws of menstruation], why not everything else? Why can't she just be a rabbi?"

Orthodox feminists are playing the game of our lives, but we have felt backed into a corner, limited to playing defense. Defensive play requires focusing purely on your opponent, not on the entire length of the court; thinking short-term, and reactively. The next generation, the next wave of Orthodox Jewish feminists, are realizing that the best defense is a good offense. On the court, it does not matter how well you block shots or steal the ball if you cannot make a basket. If we cannot shift the way we approach the problem, we will not effect change.

To be an effective change agent, we need that Zen moment of clarity to zero in on the prize: advancing the roles of women as leaders and participants in Jewish ritual.

The notion that we might emulate our Reform, Reconstructionist, and Conservative sisters has proved threatening, but until now, we have played the game defensively. When five *roshei yeshivah* (heads of the yeshivah) at Yeshiva University said that we could not pray in a women's prayer group, or when rabbis shrugged their shoulders about solving the *agunah* crisis,[1] we settled—out of political expediency, to get the "right" rabbis to support us. We had to play a lot of defense.

The next wave of Orthodox feminists will not settle. We ourselves are the facts on the ground, living examples of knowledgeable, bright, committed, and passionate women who have strong heads *on* our shoulders, but are tired of looking *over* our shoulders—that's a big no-no in basketball. We are playing offense now, and our eyes are on the prize.

We are also less concerned with the noise: the articles, blog posts, and statements that appear with regularity, naysayers who say women cannot be synagogue presidents or wear *t'fillin*; or the recent statement maintaining that the RCA (the Rabbinic Council of America) "cannot accept either the ordination of women or the recognition of women as members of the Orthodox rabbinate, regardless of the title." If we responded to such statements defensively, we would still be playing the game of politics; we prefer the offensive strategy of Jewish law and the spirit of the law. We now have the knowledge and confidence to shrug our shoulders at our opponents. We are standing on strong halachic ground.

Orthodox feminists are regularly asked the painful question, Why don't you leave, walk away, join one of the other movements? That pioneer Jewish feminist and model for us all Belda Lindenbaum (d. 2015), *zichronuh livrachah* (may her memory be a blessing), powerfully responded during her final days, "I won't leave the street, I'm not climbing into the gutter. If they want to do things they have to walk around me; I'm going to be here, and I'm going to change it." We stand firm, boldly moving forward; not looking over our shoulders and not looking back. We are playing offense, keeping our eyes on the prize: the future.

The Quietly Insistent Entrepreneur

PETER A. JOSEPH

Peter A. Joseph, a proud Wexner alumnus, is a founder, past president, and current board member of the Jewish Community Center in Manhattan. Seeing Israel as central to his Jewish identity, he is chairman emeritus of the Israel Policy Forum, an initiative that mobilizes communal leaders to support Israel's pursuit of peace and security through a negotiated settlement of the Palestinian issue. He also serves on the board of Hebrew Union College–Jewish Institute of Religion (chairing its Israel Committee), the Shalom Hartman Institute, and the New York City Citizens Budget Commission. A leader in the private equity investment business for over twenty-five years, he helped found Joseph Littlejohn & Levy (1985) and Palladium Equity Partners (1998). He now chairs Trenton Biogas LLC (TBL), a waste-to-energy project based in Trenton, New Jersey.

Following World War II, the dominant issues facing the American Jewish community related to Jewish rescue, support of the newly established State of Israel, the fight against global anti-Semitism, provision of social services, and advocacy for social justice. The sheer vastness of these concerns led to the creation of large national and international organizations commensurate with the challenges. When I joined the first New York Wexner cohort back in 1992, my understanding of leadership was predicated on the model of these organizations. First and foremost, one had to participate against the background of this large and corporate context in which, for non-professionals, what mattered most was one's donative capacity, both personally and through social networks.

As it moves well into the twenty-first century, the American Jewish community has adopted a much wider variety of communal concerns, requiring a more flexible, transparent, and responsive organizational framework. That structure dictates a new definition of effective leadership. In reflecting on my own experience as an active lay participant in Jewish communal activities, I have come to see how individual personality, character, and self-awareness (rather than donative capacity) are significant elements in advancing communal objectives.

I would describe my role as that of a quietly insistent entrepreneur, suggesting an understated but single-minded devotion to a mission. Not all entrepreneurial activity starts with a "Eureka" moment in someone's garage. Successful communal entrepreneurs may never be the originators of an initiative's seminal ideas. Rather, their skill may lay in the exercise of discerning judgment, applied to gathering and assessing other people's ideas, on the way to a deeply personal moment of self-awareness that becomes expressed as commitment.

At that point, the answer to the question of how or what one can contribute to advance the initiative in question will vary from person to person, depending on an honest self-appraisal. The idea's originator will likely need an affinity group composed of many different minds and personalities to rework the initial concept and advance it to a stage where it can generate broader interest. This is the conceptual phase of the project, which then requires financial, marketing, and other experience to give the initiative "traction." Unlike in the business sphere where ownership is a primary objective, the path to creating the "equity" of social impact is through supportive, honest and good-humored collegiality.

One element in the exercise of entrepreneurial judgment is an assessment of an initiative's potential to scale—its ability to exercise an impact beyond local self-interest. In this generative aspect of the entrepreneurial mission, what matters is the idea's generative potential, its effectiveness in spawning production and reproduction. Here, the ability to express a broader vision becomes invaluable. The engaged leader will insist at this point that the initiative be noted for quality, efficacy, and clarity of its mission, the characteristics of start-up entities that successfully garner support in a marketplace of competing initiatives.

To ensure quality, there is no substitute for strong, effective, and innovative professional management. Successful venture capitalists will tell you that partnering with talented managers is the key indicator of success, so empowering a charismatic Jewish professional who understands the mission, articulates it in a compelling manner, and creates opportunities for meaningful participation by a broad range of supporters is one of the great pleasures of quietly insistent entrepreneurship.

But exceptional professional management requires equally exceptional board oversight and governance, developed in a context of mutual respect and support. Think of boards as composed of many quietly insistent entrepreneurs, working together with enjoyment and mutual respect for one another's diverse and necessary capacities. Together, they create a culture of transparency and "best practices" governance.

Such a board requires that each of its members develop a degree of expertise in a particular area of interest. But expertise must be wed to soundness of judgment and commitment to ethical principles shared by all, regardless of particular specializations in competence. Being a well-informed, value-oriented, non-political, non-ego-driven forum sets the tone of an organization and makes it a welcome place for an ever-larger community of participants and supporters.

Throughout the process, there remains the most personal element, that indecipherable moment of self-awareness with which our engagement initially began. There is no simple formula that explains the process satisfactorily for everyone; we are all different. But in general, our relationship with Judaism and Israel, our personal family journey, our search for the gratification that comes from making a lasting mark, our concern for passing something on to our children's generation—all of these are potential elements that lead us to become involved in Jewish communal activity with passion.

Each of us, then, engages in "leadership" in our own way, consistent with our own personalities. But my concept of the quietly insistent entrepreneur encompasses a broad range of people with an equally broad range of opportunities. Our era, I believe, requires such entrepreneurship, especially in the service of smaller, creative, but generative start-ups, as opposed to the larger institutions that characterized our world in the post–World War II period. That, at least, is where I personally have derived satisfaction, and I recommend it to others who can look forward to having the rare opportunity to see some of these start-ups become a lasting legacy.

Model-Driven or Market-Driven?

A Lesson from Birthright Israel

Dr. Shaul Kelner

Shaul Kelner is associate professor of sociology and Jewish studies at Vanderbilt University, and past director of Vanderbilt's Program in Jewish Studies. He serves as chairperson of the Wexner Graduate Fellowship Selection Committee. Shaul has been a fellow of the Institute for Advanced Studies at Hebrew University of Jerusalem and the Frankel Institute for Advanced Judaic Studies at the University of Michigan, and a visiting scholar at Tel Aviv University. He lives in Nashville with his wife, Pam, and their children, Boaz and Shoshana. His book *Tours That Bind: Diaspora, Pilgrimage and Israeli Birthright Tourism* (2010) won awards from the Association for Jewish Studies and the American Sociological Association. He is currently writing a book on the Cold War-era American mobilization for Soviet Jews.

By many measures, Birthright Israel has met with remarkable success. Jewish millennials are actually *more* likely to have visited Israel than their parents, who have had many more years in which they could have found time, or made time, to take the trip.[1]

Yet as hundreds of thousands of people have returned from Israel, Jewish communal leaders continually ask, "Now what?" Engaging twenty-somethings has always been a challenge for organizations run by forty-, fifty-, and sixty-somethings. No surprise here. But by heightening expectations of what is possible with young adults, Birthright has simultaneously made failures to deliver further on those expectations all the more painful.

The steady consistency of Birthright Israel itself contrasts strikingly with the repeated launching, closing, and relaunching of successive Birthright follow-up initiatives. The reason lies not in a difference of talent or imagination. The alumni initiatives have been conceived and run by people of vision, capability, and creativity. Rather, the difference is a natural result of the fact that the approaches that Birthright Israel and Birthright follow-up initiatives take to their respective work are mirror opposites of one another.

When it was conceived in the mid-1990s, Birthright Israel began first with an educational model that was a proven success. Fifty years of experience and twenty-plus years of research had made it clear that Israel-experience programs inspire lasting connections to Israel for many and, for some, inspire major life choices as well—including careers in Jewish professional service, committed lay leadership, and aliyah.[2] As Birthright's founders saw it, the problem was that too few Jewish youth went on such programs, and those who did were mostly teenagers, not yet at the life stage where they were independently making major life decisions about career and family. Birthright's founders wanted to take this proven educational model and adapt it for a new population of young adults.

Birthright follow-up reverses the approach. Instead of starting with a commitment to an educational model and adapting it for new populations, it starts with a commitment to a target population (Birthright alumni) and then searches for models to engage them. Whereas Birthright Israel has been singularly committed to doing one thing well (providing Jewish educational travel experiences in Israel), Birthright follow-up has been consistent only in who it serves. As to the models it uses to serve this population, every few years brings a different flavor.

There are leadership lessons in the contrast between the singular consistency of Birthright Israel's *model-driven* approach and the rapid cycling of follow-up initiatives born of a *market-defined* approach. For one, we learn the importance of leaders who are staunchly committed to the value of the model itself, for its own sake, and advocate tirelessly for it. Birthright had many parents and midwives, but one would be hard-pressed to tell the story of its birth without mentioning the roles of Charles R. Bronfman and Barry Chazan: Bronfman, whose passion for Israel experience education was expressed in a decade-plus of pre-Birthright philanthropic investments to build the field; and Chazan, the educational philosopher, whose 1994 Israel experience manifesto set out an educational rationale that guided the design of Birthright's curriculum.[3]

We also learn the importance of passion for specific types of Jewish behavior. Model-driven approaches produce specific outcomes because they focus on specific actions. When advocates of Israel-experience programs are successful, people end up flying to Israel and traveling on tour buses with their peers. When advocates of family education are successful, parents end up studying at an adult level the same topics that their children are learning at a child's level. When Chabad's advocates of the Mitzvah Tank model are successful, Jews have laid *t'fillin* or lit Shabbat candles one time more than they otherwise would have. Each of these outcomes—all behaviors—are specific to themselves. None constitute the totality of Jewish life. Their proponents do not claim they do. They advocate for them because these are the behaviors that speak to their hearts.

A market-defined approach, by contrast, starts with no passion for any particular Jewish behavior; it focuses on *who* it seeks to address, not *how* it seeks to address them. Hence, it easily veers from one approach to another. Paradoxically, this flexibility in approach is part of its appeal, because it tantalizes policy makers with the notion that the target population can be engaged not partially, but totally. Market-defined approaches go hand in hand with vague concepts like "strengthening Jewish identity" and grandiose visions of "ensuring Jewish continuity" or "sparking a Jewish renaissance"—all laudable, but as the Rabbis say, *Tafasta m'rubah lo tafasta*, "If you try to catch everything, you will catch nothing."

Model-driven approaches are sometimes critiqued for "goal displacement," but this misses the fact that the behaviors in question are seen as intrinsically worthwhile, not just means to other more important ends. I find it puzzling when people ask me if Birthright trips spark greater Jewish engagement after people return home— as if the program is worth the investment only if it produces after-effects. What is not Jewish enough about simply enabling people to see the Land of Israel, a mitzvah that for millennia was the lifelong, but utterly unrealizable, dream of generations?

What if bar/bat mitzvah were evaluated as Birthright is—if the community's commitment to support bar/bat mitzvah hinged on its success in producing a desired "after-effect"? In a Boston area survey, almost half of all *b'nei mitzvah* dropped all formal Jewish engagement by senior year of high school.[4] But bar/bat mitzvah, you say, is intrinsically worthwhile, an end in itself. Precisely! And for those committed to the model-driven approaches mentioned earlier, so is traveling to Israel, studying with one's children, lay-ing *t'fillin*, and lighting Shabbat candles. The pathways to Jewish engagement are never only pathways; they are also forms of Jewish living in their own right and should be valued as such.

So much energy goes into planning programs designed for enhancing Jewish life. As those who want to lead change look to Birthright Israel as a model, they should take note: Birthright has tried two approaches to Jewish engagement. With its main pro-gram, it advocated a single, clear model of Jewish engagement. With its follow-up, it committed to doing something for a market segment. One of these approaches reshaped the Jewish world.

Student Lives on the Line

Moral Leadership in Jewish Day Schools

Rabbi Judd Kruger Levingston, PhD

Rabbi Judd Kruger Levingston, PhD, serves as director of Jewish studies at Jack M. Barrack Hebrew Academy (formerly Akiba Hebrew Academy), a community day school in Bryn Mawr, Pennsylvania. He is the author of *Sowing the Seeds of Character: The Moral Education of Adolescents in Public and Private Schools*. He lives in Northwest Philadelphia with his family, where he has served as executive vice president of education at the Germantown Jewish Centre. He is a bike-commuting and Ultimate Frisbee enthusiast.

School days are filled with moments requiring moral decisions. Here are some examples:

> Case 1: Should school leaders intervene when they know that one of their students is a target of relentless cyberbullying when she goes home every night?

> Case 2: Should a school grant a parent's wish to transfer their child to a preferred teacher even against the school's better judgment?

Case 3: Should a school give in to parent concerns that the Israeli flag out in front will make the school a target for anti-Semitic violence?

Case 4: Should a principal excuse some students from morning services because they "really hate prayer" and wish instead to use the time for private meditation or even for math homework and enrichment?

Case 5: How should the school leadership respond when an eleventh grader requests that a single-stall faculty bathroom be designated "gender-neutral" because the student is contemplating his or her gender identity?

Each of these cases offers the possibility of easy, practical solutions:

Case 1: Avoid the trauma of a disciplinary case outside of the school's jurisdiction.

Case 2: Accommodate the parent's request to change teachers—it's only one student.

Case 3: Take down the Israeli flag if it seems provocative.

Case 4: Excuse the students from prayer rather than face pushback.

Case 5: Ask the student questioning his or her identity to work things out with the school guidance counselor and help the school to avoid publicity around a bathroom change.

... And (all cases) try not to make waves, whatever happens.

Purely expedient decisions, however, may be morally misguided or even wrong. They may overlook opportunities to draw moral lessons for everyone. The cases I offer here are not just hypothetical; many schools have wrestled with these and other cases that challenge their mission and that require doing more than what is convenient.

Jewish schools seek to inspire the next generation; to create trusting, mutually supportive communities; to nurture a positive relationship with Israel; to promote academic excellence; and to guide their students' spiritual lives. They follow the commandment, first articulated in Deuteronomy 6:7 and 6:21, to teach our children to follow Judaism's moral guidelines and commandments and to remember that we were slaves in Egypt who were fortunate to have been set free. These commandments are not obsolete: they command us to develop our students' identities, sense of responsibility, and moral character as we would do for our own children.

We might be tempted to limit our mandate to educating the mind, but surely we should strive for more. Seeing our students eight hours a day for at least 160 school days each year puts us in a quasi-parenting role. If a student's gender, religious, or ethnic identity is criticized, compromised, or bullied—usually by students but sometimes by teachers too—we are responsible. Whether the student identifies as BGLQT or as Sephardi, Israeli, Russian, Ashkenazi, or "culturally Jewish," the school leadership should find ways, including disciplinary consequences if necessary, to intervene positively on the student's behalf. We extend our concern about feeling at home to everyone; nobody should feel less legitimate or less authentic than anybody else.

Even if bullying takes place off-campus, if it involves students from the school and if the bullies touch on issues that arise in school or in the extended school community, then the school can and should intervene. The relatively high rate of suicide among teenagers struggling with their identities should remind us of our job to keep the Jewish tent wide open and to foster respect for all who seek to be inside.

We can stretch students of any age to think through moral issues in the curriculum from the ethics of medicine (end-of-life issues), to economics (income distribution), arts (freedom of expression), professional sports (winning at all costs), science (nuclear power), and other fields. Ethical issues arise for administrators wrestling with the kinds of cases with which I began this essay and with other cases too—such as grouping our students by ability, sharing disciplinary histories with people outside of our schools, and in describing and promoting our students in the college admissions process.

Schools whose statements of mission speak to the moral value of citizenship have an obligation to discuss ethics in politics, to encourage students to vote, to ask what it might mean to serve in the military, and even to ask what we would be willing to give up to be counted as Jews. Believing that we are inextricably intertwined with the modern State of Israel, we should fly the Israeli flag, send out students there, support meaningful exchange programs, and learn the narratives that are part of the nation's history. Israel education is a serious enterprise for young people of any age, and it always helps to have some good falafel, hummus, and rugelach pastries to raise the energy of a program and to bring people of different views together.

Empathy can inform moral leadership; we must empathize with our parents who entrust their children to our care all week long, and we also must empathize with our students who are in our care. This level of empathy means that we don't always have to have answers. Sometimes we can be most effective by lending an ear and by offering moral reflection; sometimes parents or students require us to remind them of our mission so that they see themselves as part of the larger whole.

Each year at graduation, we can ask students to wrestle with moral questions of adulthood, such as "What will be my legacy?" or "How will I leave my sheltered life at school for the wider world?" Just raising such questions acknowledges the ultimate goals of preparing students to lead rich moral lives. We should be satisfied with nothing less. After all, our students' lives are on the line.

PART THREE

Appreciation

Les Wexner, Harry Truman, and the Leadership of Readership

David Gergen

David Gergen is a professor of public service and co-director of the Center for Public Leadership at Harvard's John F. Kennedy School of Government, where he works closely with a rising generation of leaders, especially social entrepreneurs, military veterans, and Young Global Leaders chosen by the World Economic Forum. Starting with the *MacNeil-Lehrer News Hour* in 1984, he has been a regular commentator on public affairs and is now senior political analyst for CNN. He has served as White House adviser to four US presidents of both parties: Nixon, Ford, Reagan, and Clinton—experiences he has described in his *New York Times* best-seller *Eyewitness to Power: The Essence of Leadership, Nixon to Clinton* (2001). He has been married since 1967 to Anne Elizabeth Gergen of England, a family therapist. They have two children and five grandchildren.

Harry Truman was the only American president of the twentieth century who never went to college. When he graduated from high school, his parents were experiencing hard times, and Harry went to work, eventually spending seven years plowing fields behind a mule.

Yet Truman turned out to be one of our wisest leaders, getting most of the big decisions right as World War II ended and the Cold War opened. He believed that a lifetime of reading biographies and histories made the difference. When I visited his presidential library a few years ago—one of the last built with modesty—I found a copy of a talk he gave to high school students visiting him. "Not every reader is a leader," he said, "but every leader must be a reader."

Harry Truman would have loved Leslie Wexner.

In my first extended conversation with Les and Abigail, I was a guest in their home for a small dinner, and I was struck by the parallels. While Les had the privilege of an undergraduate education at the Ohio State University, it was immediately apparent that like Truman, he was a self-educated man who had spent years voraciously reading and learning about leadership from biographies and histories.

At that dinner, the conversation turned to the early days of the republic, and Les started talking about George Washington. He didn't simply know a little about Washington; he knew tons. I had never met anyone who had read all seven volumes of Douglas Southall Freeman's magisterial biography of Washington, much less the four-volume biography by James Flexner. Les had read all those and more—and he talked knowledgeably about how Washington at first stumbled as general of the Continental army, losing six of his first eight battles. Instead of quitting, as Les pointed out, Washington grew into a smarter, better leader, changing to a guerilla-style general. The Revolutionary War eventually became Britain's Vietnam, and Washington emerged as the most respected leader in America until Lincoln.

Since that first memorable dinner, Les has sent me—along with others—a stream of new books that he has devoured and thinks I should read. They tend to be about major American political figures—Jefferson, Madison, Hamilton, Lincoln, Teddy Roosevelt, FDR, George H. W. Bush—but often they focus on generals—Napoleon, Lee, Marshall, MacArthur. He is fascinated by World War II and the nigh-incomprehensible rise of the Third Reich, especially in contrast to the courage of the British people and the extraordinary leadership of Churchill. Think of a contemporary author of history and biography—Doris Kearns Goodwin, David McCullough, Thomas Friedman, David Brooks—and I can assure you he has read at least one by each; in the case of Goodwin, he seems to have read them all.

When I recently saw him, Les was deeply into Niall Ferguson's long, first-volume portrait of Kissinger as well as Jon Meacham's new biography of George H. W. Bush and a portrait of Brent Scowcroft as a geopolitical strategist. Before Robert Gates and Leon Panetta visited Columbus, Ohio, for public appearances in recent years, Les had finished their recent memoirs. Before he brought Tony Blair to Harvard, he had read Blair's memoir. Someone recently gave me a copy of *The Boys in the Boat*, a book with which I was unfamiliar. I thought, "Aha, now I finally have a chance to turn the tables, introducing Les to a book he doesn't know." Over dinner in Columbus, I asked him if he had ever heard of it. His answer: Of course, I have read it, so has Abigail, and so has my son David (the rower). "It's wonderful." I didn't have the guts to say that it was still unread on my shelves.

It has become increasingly apparent to me that the whole Wexner household is made up of bibliophiles. In their family rooms, books are piled up everywhere. Not long ago, I was in their kitchen at a breakfast table. There, stacked up neatly, were four books that had just arrived from Amazon. "Who is reading these?" I asked. It turned out that each book was for a different member of the family.

Les and I have shared fewer books about Israel and Judaism, but each time I visit Abigail House, I see new books about them that he is studying. The visit by Shimon Peres for the thirtieth anniversary of The Wexner Foundation revealed, I thought, how deeply Les has absorbed the lessons of Jewish history. They go to the core of his being.

Anyone who knows Les understands how much he also appreciates good books that focus on leadership and management. He has not only read Peter Drucker but has dug extensively into the works of Warren Bennis, James MacGregor Burns, John Gardner, Bill George, Stan McChrytstal, John Kotter, and John Wooden. These days he frequently cites passages from more recent works by Max Bazerman, Ron Heifetz, and Chris Zook.

What Les has discovered is what Truman and many others have found: that a close reading of the past can yield a profound understanding of human nature, the forces that move nations and peoples, and how individual leaders have bent those forces to advance humankind—or, as Steve Jobs once put it, to "put a dent in the universe." A close reading also persuades many, like Truman, to believe that men and women are not slaves to history, as Tolstoy thought, but shapers of history, as Carlyle thought.

For reflective leaders, reading is not an idle exercise. They see it as a smart way of informing their judgment and making better decisions. I well recall one weekend when Oprah Winfrey visited Les and Abigail to talk about the best way to set up a philanthropic foundation. Two or three of us were invited to join the conversation. Les responded that before creating The Wexner Foundation, he read the biographies of great philanthropists of the past such as Andrew Carnegie, Andrew Mellon, and John D. Rockefeller. Each of them offered lessons from the past still applicable in our new era.

Since the beginning of the republic, America's public leaders have drawn heavily upon their readings of history, biography, philosophy, and science to shape their judgments. Could Madison possibly have been the father of the Constitution without a keen appreciation of the past? Would the Federalist papers even have existed? As John Gardner points out in *On Leadership*, one of the finest books in the genre:

> Our Founding Fathers had varying levels of formal education but through reading they shared the best thought of the ages. They knew Plutarch and Thucydides. They had read and discussed Bacon, Hume, Locke and Montesquieu. And they were deeply interested in the science of their day—incomparably more interested than American leaders today.[1]

Lincoln had access to only a small number of books on the prairie, but his close reading of them were enormously influential. In his book *Lincoln: The Biography of a Writer*, Fred Kaplan describes a twelve-year-old Lincoln discovering biography for the first time. He was captivated by Benjamin Franklin's autobiography and Parson Weems's *Life of Washington*. As Kaplan writes, Franklin's Horatio Alger story gave value to Lincoln's own, vaunting ambition; he, too, could rise in the world. For the young boy, "Washington's deification as the father of his country provided a model of bipartisan patriotism, the gentleman-soldier whose temperament stressed rational prudence."[2]

It was not just white males who have benefited through history. Indeed, literature has long been a force for liberation and social justice. Shining shoes on the docks of Baltimore in the nineteenth century, a young slave boy overheard some privileged white kids talking about a primer on oratory they were studying at school. The shoe-shine boy decided he wanted it too. So, he saved up his pennies, bought a copy, and studied it assiduously. That young boy grew up to be Frederick Douglass, one of the finest orators in American history. Not many years later, a father in mid-America offered to pay his young daughter fifty cents for every portrait by Plutarch she read. She took up the challenge on the way to becoming one of the best leaders the country has ever known: Jane Addams.

On this remembrance of the thirtieth anniversary of The Wexner Foundation and this celebration of Les Wexner and his wonderful family, it might be best to close by returning to Truman.

When Franklin Roosevelt died from a stroke in 1945, Americans weren't at all sure Truman was up to the presidency; nor was he. One solace that citizens had was Truman's decision to surround himself with some of the finest public servants in the nation's history. Truman might be out of his depth, the thinking went, but those big people around him could set him straight.

As experienced leaders know, there is only one problem with that little theory: what in the world happens if advisers to the leader are split? And in the presidency, that occurs far more often than one might think. After all, only the really tough decisions make it to the Oval Office, so questions are often a 51–49 call. Or even closer. It is then up to the president to reach deep inside himself and—alone—make the decision.

That's exactly what happened after World War II when the question arose for Truman whether the United States should officially bless and nurture a new homeland for the Jews in Palestine, as promised decades earlier in the Balfour Declaration. Truman's top advisers were sharply and deeply split. George Marshall, Truman's secretary of state and the most respected man in America, along with most of "the wise men" of the time, were vehemently against the United States taking a lead in promoting a Jewish state; they worried that war would break out with Arabs, who vastly outnumbered Jews, and a cutoff of oil would devastate Europe, spreading communism across the continent. On the other side, Truman's top domestic adviser, Clark Clifford, as well as others in the White House, just as vehemently believed that the president should help to father a new Jewish state because it was morally the right decision and was consistent with American values. His team divided, Truman had to go deep into his soul to find the answer.

As recounted by Michael Benson (*Harry S. Truman and the Founding of Israel*), Truman soon showed what he was made of. In 1946, several cabinet officers along with military generals gathered in the Oval Office to talk about what future the United States wanted for the Middle East. One of them, Dwight Eisenhower, wasn't sure Truman "understood the consequences" of Middle East policies. As Benson writes:

> Truman opened up a desk drawer and took out a large map of the eastern Mediterranean, the Middle East, and central and southern Asia.... Unfolding the map on his desk, Truman then proceeded to give a 15-minute dissertation on the historical importance and present-day strategic significance of the area, which at least one person present described later as "masterful."[3]

Two years later, after a climactic and storied showdown between George Marshall and Clark Clifford, Truman made the call: the

United States—flying in the face of opinion almost everywhere in the world—came down firmly on the side of recognizing Israel. It was a courageous decision, one of the most difficult a president has made. It was also a wise one, drawn upon his self-obtained knowledge of the Middle East and his deep, continuous reading of the Bible.

Truman always believed that readers of good books, especially biographies and histories, were preparing themselves for leadership. For him, as he recounted, reading "was far more than a romantic adventure. It was solid instruction and wise teaching, which I somehow felt that I wanted and needed."[4] Can't you just see Les Wexner nodding vigorously in agreement?

Les Wexner and the Polar Bears

Charles R. Bronfman

Charles R. Bronfman, PC, CC, founded the Andrea and Charles Bronfman Philanthropies in 1985. He is the former co-chairman of the Seagram Company Limited, founding owner of the Montreal Expos, and former chairman of Koor Industries (Israel). His major philanthropic thrusts include Historica-Canada, The McGill Institute for the Study of Canada, and Birthright Israel. He is the recipient of honorary degrees from universities in Canada, the United States, and Israel. In June 1992 he was made a companion of the Order of Canada and in July of the same year became a member of Her Majesty's Privy Council for Canada.

I first met Leslie Wexner at what has been referred to as the "breakfast of champions," that United Jewish Appeal (UJA) event that raised $54 million from a small number of major contributors for Operation Exodus, the effort to move Jews from the former Soviet Union to Israel and elsewhere. Shortly thereafter, the then CEO of UJA, Brian Lurie, asked Les and me to co-chair a study group of mega-donors to Jewish life. At that breakfast he noticed that hardly any of the attendees were acquainted. He realized that in the event of another crisis or opportunity it would be well if they knew one another well.

While Les and I came from different communities and grew up in different businesses, we shared a passion for philanthropy, leadership, and enhancing Jewish life in North America and in Israel. For the better part of the next decade, Les and I co-chaired the "Study Group," euphemistically known as the "Mega Group." Les called it the Polar Bear Club, based on the thesis that polar bears like walking around, checking each other out, but never truly bonding. The metaphor was true only to a point, because even though few of us knew one another at the group's launching, many became business and philanthropic partners as it evolved.

Among the interesting dynamics that ultimately led to the group's demise was the inability to attain alignment on the question of whether we ought to work together on big Jewish issues. Les was a tireless advocate of the maximalist position held by one-third of the group: that each member should commit to an eight-figure gift, so as to create a pool of $100 million plus for innovative approaches to contemporary Jewish challenges. The third of the group that frustrated Les the most were the minimalists, who outright rejected partnering with others, insisting instead on acting alone as they felt moved by this or that Jewish need. A middle third picked and chose those initiatives for which they were prepared to make collaborative mega-commitments. Despite its internal differences, however, the group as a whole has had considerable impact. It was largely responsible for the early funding of such initiatives as the rescue of Hillel after its spin-off from B'nai B'rith, the initiation of the Partnership for Excellence in Jewish Education (PEJE), and the launch of Birthright Israel.

Les and I shared something else as well: each of us founded a private foundation to pursue philanthropic concerns. For Les, it was a single-minded focus on leadership development, for which I congratulate him, both for the dazzling foresight that he showed in conceptualizing it and for carrying it through so brilliantly. At the same time, the two of us collaborated particularly closely because more than other North American Jewish philanthropists, we were intimately involved in supporting and leading the disparate entities of the "organized Jewish community" that were considering a merger.

In 1999, after seven long years of negotiations, United Jewish Appeal, the Council of Jewish Federations, and the United Israel

Appeal were finally ready to combine, and the two of us devoted both our time and our treasury to making the merger work. Feeling that too much attention had been paid to structure and governance with little focus on function, Les even assembled the leaders of these three organizations to his headquarters in Columbus, Ohio, where one of his corporate consulting firms helped them look at vision, mission, and operating plans. Les and I were totally aligned on the strategic imperative that this merger could represent and hoped that the combination would help frame the organized Jewish community for a twenty-first-century resurgence. I became the initial chairman of the entity that resulted—newly named the United Jewish Communities—and Les was prepared to follow me in that position. Regrettably for the Jewish community, this was not to be, as the issue that Les had raised—what exactly the organization was going to do—was never successfully resolved and continues to haunt the organization to this day.

My final example of Les's leadership is the one that I hold most dear. As a longtime believer in Israel travel for the building of Jewish identity and enhancing connections between Israel and the Jewish world, I was privileged, with Michael Steinhardt, to found Birthright Israel, whose success has been far beyond any of our dreams. When Les came to Jerusalem to accept an honorary doctorate from the Hebrew University, Andy, my late wife, and I invited him and Abigail to lunch at our foundation's offices. Both his and my advisers had been discussing the possibility of Les becoming a founding donor to Birthright. After considerable discussion, they agreed among themselves that the timing was not yet right and that I should not solicit Les at that lunch. But Les and I were having such an extraordinarily good time at the lunch talking about the things that we love that, even with all the advisers present, I couldn't help but ignore their advice and ask Les to join as one of the original fourteen $5 million donors to Birthright. Les immediately said he would be delighted to. He then asked a few minutes later whether I knew why he chose to make the gift. As I didn't, he explained that he has an appreciation of leadership; this project represented Michael and me stepping forward as leaders, and he wanted to support that type of leadership in the Jewish community.

All these many years later, Les continues to support Birthright Israel, as he does so much of importance in Jewish life. I am proud to consider him a friend and wish him many more years of satisfaction and leadership as he goes about changing the Jewish world. He is a role model of bold leadership in philanthropy, as in business—in fact, in all that he does.

Leadership

The Most Important Topic

LESLIE WEXNER

Leslie H. Wexner is the chairman and CEO of L Brands, which he founded with a $5,000 loan in 1963. He is the longest serving CEO in America and has earned the highest total shareholder return of any current CEO worldwide. Mr. Wexner has a profound interest in the development of tomorrow's leaders. He is a member of the American Academy of Arts and Sciences, chairman of the Ohio State University Wexner Medical Center Board, chairman of the advisory council for the Center for Public Leadership at Harvard University, a member of the Royal Shakespeare Company International Council, the chairman of the Columbus Partnership, and founder and co-chair, with his wife, of The Wexner Foundation. He has twice been chairman of the board of Ohio State University and is the founding member and first chair of the Ohio State University Foundation. Mr. Wexner and his wife, Abigail, are the parents of four children.

One of my favorite quotes to repeat to my children, originally attributed to President Truman, is "Not all readers are leaders, but all leaders are readers." You will see in these remarks how reading about great leaders has informed my understanding of what I believe to be the most important subject. Let me explain how I arrived at that conclusion.

I started my business in my mid-twenties with a $5,000 loan from my aunt Ida. In those early years I was incredibly insecure. I was more afraid to fail than I was motivated to succeed. That gut-twisting fear fueled me to work one-hundred-plus-hour weeks every week—to keep my nose as hard pressed to the grindstone as I could. I literally developed a stress-induced stomach ulcer. As the saying goes, though, "If you keep your nose to the grindstone long enough, soon you will have no nose." About a decade after I started my business—in my mid-thirties—I had a moment of clarity when I realized I was more successful on paper than I ever imagined I could be. And I was profoundly unhappy. Up to that point my entire worldview was based on a singular desire not to be poor—to have agency over my life. From the time I was a little boy shoveling snow in the winter and mowing lawns in the summer, work was the vehicle that would allow me to break free from the constraints my parents experienced. I was blessed to be born in a country and time when hard work and determination could pay off. When it did, when I began to achieve the success I always dreamed of, I realized I had to deliberately rethink how I saw the world. And so the work of searching for my purpose began.

The first thing I needed to do was learn about how aspiring leaders organized their thinking. Before that time, I had never read anything I didn't have to—and there were probably things I was told to read that I didn't. I started with biographies. Learning about the greatest leaders in history—Washington, Lincoln, Churchill—broadened my perspective. This began a lifelong habit of reading. Since then, I haven't read less than fifty books per year. I don't say that to be boastful, but rather to emphasize that I take learning seriously. Reading is not something I do once a year at the beach. It's something I deliberately make time for every day. One of the things I learned from my reading, and subsequently tried to practice, is that leaders lead themselves first. Everyone has an internal monologue, but very few people *lead* themselves. Around this time, Abraham Zaleznik, Harvard Business School professor, told me, "The highest-risk person in your organization is you." That lesson had a profound influence on me, and I return to it often. The problem is never *them*, it's always *me*. Indeed, one of the reasons I am so emphatic in my insistence on reading is that it is both a way to learn to lead and is itself a practice of self-leadership.

In reading about the most successful businesspeople in history—Rockefeller, Carnegie, the Rothschilds, the Warburgs—I started to think about how to most effectively give back. Something I understood from my business career was that "focusing on a lot of things" is a contradiction of terms. *At most*, I think we are capable of focusing on three things. After years of reflection, I decided the things I cared most about and could impact were my local community in Ohio, the Jewish community, and my alma mater. One of my basic philosophical beliefs is that I have a responsibility to my local community. How can I devote time and resources to a distant cause and neglect issues close to home? In a sense, the same logic applied to making Jewish philanthropy one of my priorities. At the time, the Jewish People were emerging from a series of horrific crises. I felt, and still feel, that it is my responsibility to take care of my larger Jewish family. Just as I had struggled personally to establish agency over my life, I wanted to do my part to make sure the Jewish People would never again be powerless victims. Finally, I came to appreciate that, but for Ohio State, I never would have been able to go to college. I owe my alma mater a tremendous debt of gratitude.

I was blessed during this period to find wise mentors. Around the time I was forty, I was put in charge of soliciting major international gifts for United Jewish Appeal (UJA). It was in that capacity that I met Rabbi David Hartman. One Shabbat afternoon in Jerusalem I took a walk with Rabbi Hartman and asked him to teach me Talmud. I was prepared to take time off work in the summer to study with him. To my surprise, he refused, saying I didn't need to. He explained that he believed I had a moral compass and that my talent was seeing patterns. I should, he suggested, focus on problems facing Israel and the Jewish world and try to fill an unmet need. At the time, I was both flattered and suspicious that he didn't think I had the intellect to be a great student. With the benefit of hindsight, I understand Rabbi Hartman's wisdom. Certainly he valued studying Talmud—he devoted his life to it. Indeed, Rabbi

Hartman was an esteemed leader in his field. He had the judgment, however, to recognize that his path was not for everyone. He recognized in me talents I could continue to hone for the greater good. I never would have led in Talmudic study, but I could be a leader.

As I began to think about setting up a foundation, I took inspiration from Rockefeller and decided the foundation should be led by a rabbi. The historian and author of *Leadership*, James MacGregor Burns, explains the lesson that leadership is always built on the bedrock of values. Hitler was a horrendous leader because he was morally bankrupt and, in spite of his popularity, left his community worse off. I am proud to be a member of a faith that values *tikkun olam*—repairing the world, seeking justice, and defending the downtrodden. I wanted The Wexner Foundation to be led by someone with a moral compass informed by *timeless* and *sacred* values.

In continued conversations with Rabbi Hartman and other mentors, I began to see the pattern that the Jewish community was not adequately training and supporting leaders. In my work with UJA I met Jewish leaders, but it seemed to me that very few people were talking about what leadership really meant, let alone *Jewish leadership* as a distinct category. And so I set out, with a deep and abiding belief that people matter, to do my small part to bring the subject of Jewish leadership to the fore.

After thirty years of The Wexner Foundation's work, work without a political agenda or specific end goal in mind, I am more convinced than ever that leadership can be taught—that it *must* be taught. The future of the Jewish People, and of the world, depends on cultivating strong, moral, effective leaders.

Great thinkers, many of whom contributed to this book, have devoted themselves to developing a leadership curriculum. They are far more qualified than I to comment on *how* to teach leadership. From my own experience, however, I know that regardless of the degree to which you think leadership is nature or nurture, leadership is apt to lay dormant if it is not cultivated. Had I not been blessed with wise mentors, had I not had the opportunity to go to college at Ohio State, I would never have developed whatever capacity for leadership I have.

It is also an undeniable reality that leadership must be largely self-taught. Anyone with a rudimentary knowledge of history knows Lincoln struggled to learn anything and everything he could from reading borrowed books by candlelight. But on the other hand, look at Churchill, who was born into tremendous privilege. Churchill was, by his own admission, a terrible student who failed to get into Sandhurst multiple times. It wasn't until his twenties, not coincidentally when he started to take it upon himself to read history, that Churchill really developed his mind and his abilities as a leader. Put simply, all the resources in the world won't teach someone who doesn't want to be taught. Our challenge, then, is twofold: to provide resources to cultivate leaders *and* to encourage the next generation to take up the mantle of leadership for themselves. And, crucially, this must be balanced with the fundamental insight that nothing matters unless I commit to lead myself in a moral, thoughtful way.

Finally, and most importantly, the development of leaders must be rooted in an understanding of practical challenges. Leaders come in all shapes and sizes and lead in different ways, but all leaders do the doing. In my twenties, I was too concerned with going full speed ahead all the time to be a thoughtful leader. The balance I struggle to strike is between taking time to reflect while always keeping execution in mind. None of our hard work will matter if we ever forget that "leadership" is a verb.

CONCLUSION

Ten Commandments for Leaders

RABBI LAWRENCE A. HOFFMAN, PHD

Rabbi Lawrence A. Hoffman, PhD, is the Barbara and Stephen Fried-man Professor of Liturgy, Worship and Ritual at the Hebrew Union College–Jewish Institute of Religion in New York. In 1995, he co-founded Synagogue 2000, dedicated to transforming synagogues into spiritual and moral centers for the twenty-first century. He has writ-ten or edited over forty books, including *Rethinking Synagogues* and (co-edited) *Sacred Strategies: Transforming Synagogues from Functional to Visionary*. He is the recipient of two National Jewish Book Awards, two honorary doctorates, the Abraham Geiger Medal (from the Abraham Geiger Rabbinic School in Berlin), and the *Berakah* Award for lifetime achievement (from the North American Academy of Liturgy). He is a regular speaker, lecturer, and consultant for synagogues worldwide.

What the Jewish People do *not* need is another example of yesteryear's salvage operations—saving Jewish literacy, Jewish memories, Jewish in-marriage, Jewish nostalgia, or Jewish anything-else. We require, instead, a passionate commitment to leadership that is rooted Jewishly, imagines daringly, thinks cre-atively, and acts strategically—not to recoup past losses, but to establish future gains. With proper leadership, we can be for our time what the Rabbis were for life under Rome, what Maimonides was for the golden age of medieval philosophy, and what Zionists were for that window of opportunity that gave us just the third Jewish commonwealth in all of history.

Precisely that is the vision of this book, the vision of The Wexner Foundation for the past thirty years. I came more fully to appreciate it as I myself looked back upon joining the Wexner faculty almost at the beginning and realized how much it had changed me. No longer just the ivory-tower scholar that my doctoral education assumed, I became someone aspiring to leadership myself, in pursuit of Judaism's dream of a better tomorrow—not just in God's good time but in real time, convinced that Jewish wisdom and insightful leadership might get us there.

Any Torah of leadership ought to have its own Ten Commandments—not the be-all and end-all of leadership, certainly (it takes a whole Torah for that), but a shorthand list of things worth remembering, as we awaken each day with Judaism's prescribed note of grateful acknowledgment on our lips: *Modeh/modah ani* ..., "I am grateful, I acknowledge ... that You, God, have returned my soul to me"—that I may lead the life of promise for which I am created.

Here, then, are my own personal "Ten Commandments of Leadership" to be emblazoned on the boardroom walls of every Jewish organization and the computer screen savers of everyone who works there:

1. Attack tomorrow's challenges, not yesterday's. Be optimistic, not pessimistic; proactive, not reactive.
2. If we demonstrate the reason Judaism matters, it will start to matter.
3. Develop a compelling vision of why and how it ought to matter, and remain true to that vision.
4. Root the vision in a strong moral compass; be value-driven—with guiding values that are inherently Jewish but intensely universal as well.
5. Saturate your organization with that strong moral leadership buttressed by authentic Jewish learning.
6. Run your organization with consummate creative excellence. Your mission is too serious to let it be compromised

by mediocrity. Demand excellence for yourself, and get it from others. Avoid bureaucratic sclerosis, the natural tendency of organizations to override creative excellence with rules well followed for no other reason than that they are rules. Instead of an automatic "No," try risking a "Maybe yes."

7. Treat everyone with respect: your own staff, the workers and consultants you hire, the people you serve—those who put their faith in you. Do everything you can to show everyone you meet how much they matter.

8. Practice scrupulous honesty, with regular reviews of what is working and what is not. Do whatever is necessary to reestablish the centrality of your vision and the excellence of how you carry it out.

9. Surround yourself with the right people: they must share your values and your vision; they must do, with excellence, what you cannot do yourself; and they must work positively as a team, with faith in what you all are building together.

10. Over time, these practices will build trust—trust well-placed, trust that will catapult everyone to a place of demanding the best from themselves and enjoying the common journey to a better future.

▲ ▲▼▲ ▲▼▲ ▲▼▲ ▲▼▲ ▲

NOTES

Introduction: Leadership and the Jewish Condition, by Rabbi Lawrence A. Hoffman, PhD

1. Rich Karlgaard, "Peter Drucker on Leadership," *Forbes*, November, 19, 2004, http://www.forbes.com/2004/11/19/cz_rk_1119drucker.html.
2. Warren Bennis, *On Becoming a Leader: The Leadership Classic*, rev. ed. (New York: Basic Books, 2009), xxix.
3. Barbara Kellerman, *The End of Leadership* (New York: HarperCollins, 2012), 156.

Nudging as a Tool of Leaders, by Dr. Max H. Bazerman

1. L. L. Shu, N. Mazar, F. Gino, D. Ariely, and M. H. Bazerman, "Signing at the Beginning Makes Ethics Salient and Decreases Dishonest Self-Reports in Comparison to Signing at the End," *Proceedings of the National Academy of Sciences* 109, no. 38 (2011): 15197–200.
2. Richard H. Thaler and Cass R. Sunstein, *Nudge: Improving Decisions About Health, Wealth, and Happiness* (New Haven, CT: Yale University Press, 2008); Daniel Kahneman, *Thinking, Fast and Slow* (New York: Farrar, Straus and Giroux, 2011).

The Power of Inclusion, by Patricia Bellinger

1. Mahzarin Banaji and Tony Greenwald, *Blind Spot: Hidden Biases of Good People* (New York: Delacorte Press, 2013), 208, 187.
2. Ibid., xv.
3. Claudia Goldin and Cecilia Rouse, "Orchestrating Impartiality: The Impact of 'Blind' Auditions on Female Musicians," (working paper no. 5903, National Bureau of Economic Research 1997), www.nber.org/papers/w5903.
4. See GapJumpers, www.gapjumpers.me.
5. Kenji Yoshino and Christie Smith, *Uncovering Talent: A New Model of Inclusion* (Westlake, TX: Deloitte University Leadership Center for Inclusion, 2013).
6. Ibid., 3.
7. Ibid., 12.

Leading So You Get It Wrong, by Dr. Anna Poupko Fisher

1. Ludwig Wittgenstein (1889–1951), *Tractatus Logico-Philosophicus* (1922; repr., New York: Cosimo Books, 2007), 3:01. This small treatise, a rigorous analysis of the logic of language and reality, was composed in the trenches of World War I and became the basis of Wittgenstein's being

given a doctorate and professorship alongside Bertrand Russell and G. E. Moore at Cambridge University. An engineer by training, with a degree in aeronautics, Wittgenstein also dabbled in inventions. His earliest, at the age of ten, was a sewing machine fashioned out of spare wooden parts.

2. Bertrand Russell, introduction to ibid., 18.
3. Wittgenstein, *Tractatus Logico-Philosophicus*, 3:13.
4. Ibid., 5:621.
5. Russell, introduction, 18.
6. Wittgenstein, *Tractatus Logico-Philosophicus*, 6:54.

Jewish Adaptability, Authority, and Leadership, by Ronald Heifetz
1. Gidi Grinstein, *Flexigidity: The Secret of Jewish Adaptability* (Tel Aviv: Reut Institute, 2014).
2. Rodger Kamenetz, *The Jew in the Lotus: A Poet's Rediscovery of Jewish Identity in Buddhist India* (San Francisco: HarperSanFrancisco, 1994).
3. Ronald Heifetz, *Leadership Without Easy Answers* (Cambridge, MA: Belknap Press of Harvard University Press, 1994), 2.

The Heart of Darkness, by Dr. Barbara Kellerman
1. Hannah Arendt, *Totalitarianism: Part Three of Origins of Totalitarianism* (San Diego: Harcourt, Brace & World, 1968), 71.
2. James MacGregor Burns, *Leadership* (New York: Harper & Row, 1978), 18.
3. Barbara Kellerman, "Hitler's Ghost: A Manifesto," in *Cutting Edge: Leadership 2000*, by Barbara Kellerman and Larraine Matusak (College Park: University of Maryland, 2000), 68.

Leaders and Managers: Divergence and Convergence, by Larry Moses
1. Warren G. Bennis, "Managing the Dream: Leadership in the 21st Century," *Journal of Organizational Change and Management* 2, no. 1 (1989): 7; Warren G. Bennis and Burt Nanus, *Leaders: The Strategies for Taking Charge* (New York: HarperCollins, 2007), 20.
2. Alan Murray, *The Wall Street Journal Essential Guide to Management* (New York: Harper Business, 2010).

What Do You Stand For?, by Dr. Erica Brown
1. Jeffrey H. Tigay, *The JPS Torah Commentary: Deuteronomy* (Philadelphia: Jewish Publication Society, 1996).

First Plant the Sapling: Beyond Messianic Leadership, by Rabbi Lisa J. Grushcow, DPhil
1. Talmud, *Gittin* 56a–b.
2. Tomas Chamorro-Premuzic, "Why Do So Many Incompetent Men Become Leaders?," *Harvard Business Review*, August 22, 2013, https://hbr.org /2013/08/why-do-so-many-incompetent-men, cited in a conversation on Wexnet in October 2015.
3. Ibid.

4. Gary Rosenblatt, "Where Are Tomorrow's Leaders?," *Jewish Week*, October 7, 2015, www.thejewishweek.com/editorial-opinion/gary-rosenblatt /where-are-tomorrows-leaders#3MAgtSsY4WLM4VbO.99.
5. See Aaron Panken, *The Rhetoric of Innovation* (Lanham: University Press of America, 2005), 189–92.
6. After his death, a great many other things are attributed to him in retrospect. See Lisa Grushcow, *Writing the Wayward Wife* (Leiden: Brill, 2006), 233–39.
7. *Avot d'Rabbi Natan* 31.

Solidarity Ethnic and Human: Moses and Moral Responsibility, by Rabbi Shai Held, PhD

1. This essay expands upon my "Why Moses? Or: What Makes a Leader," forthcoming in *The Heart of Torah* (Philadelphia: Jewish Publication Society, 2017).
2. "'Hebrew' is frequently used by non-Israelites to describe an Israelite, as when Egyptians call Joseph a Hebrew (Potiphar's wife, Genesis 39:14,17; Pharaoh's cupbearer, 41:12), or when the Philistines refer to the Israelites in Samuel's day (1 Samuel 4:6)." Bill T. Arnold, *Genesis* (New York: Cambridge University Press, 2009), 147.
3. See Gili Zivan, "The Secret of Compassion" in Hebrew, *Amudim*, Iyar–Sivan 2012, 21–23.
4. Peter Enns, *Exodus* (Grand Rapids: Zondervan, 2000), 452.

The God Who Loves Pluralism, by Rabbi Rachel Sabath Beit-Halachmi, PhD

1. David Hartman, *A Heart of Many Rooms* (Woodstock: Jewish Lights, 1999), 21–23.

Marshmallows, Ketchup, and Redemption: How Leaders Manage Expectations, by Rabbi Jacob J. Schacter, PhD

1. *Exodus Rabbah* 3:14; *Leviticus Rabbah* 11:6.
2. *Pirkei d'Rabbi Eliezer* 40.
3. Maimonides, *Epistle to Yemen*.

Judge Away, by Rabbi Shira Stutman

1. *Genesis Rabbah* 12:15.

Leadership and Confrontation: Lessons from Moses and God, by Rabbi Melissa Weintraub

1. *Exodus Rabbah* 42:10; Rashi ad loc.
2. *Pesikta Rabbati* 40.

Keep It Simple: The Three Stages of Change, by Rabbi Avi Weiss

1. *Genesis Rabbah* 42:13.
2. Rashi to Exodus 5:1.

"Let What Is Broken So Remain": Leadership's Lotus Hour, by Rabbi Mishael Zion

1. Rabbi Moshe Chalfon HaCohen (1874–1950), *Darkhei Moshe*, commentary to *Sh'mot*.
2. Ibid.

The Jewish People's Story, Not Just My Own, by Dr. Deborah E. Lipstadt

1. Deborah E. Lipstadt, *Denying the Holocaust: The Growing Assault on Truth and Memory*.

Stop Feeling Sorry for Disabled Children (Start Respecting Them Instead), by Dr. Maurit Beeri

1. *Mishnah Avot* 1:14.

Out of the Shtetl: A Mature, Confident, and Constructive Zionism, by Nadav Tamir

1. Ronald A. Heifetz, *Leadership Without Easy Answers* (Cambridge, MA: Belknap Press of Harvard University Press, 1994).
2. Dan Senor and Saul Singer, *Start-Up Nation: The Story of Israel's Economic Miracle* (New York: Twelve, 2009).
3. See Marshall Ganz, "Why Stories Matter: The Arts and Craft of Social Change," *Sojourners*, March 2009, 16–21.
4. Roger Fisher, William L. Ury, and Bruce Patton, *Getting to Yes: Negotiating Agreement Without Giving In* (New York: Houghton Mifflin, 2011).
5. Joseph S. Nye Jr., *Soft Power: The Means to Success in World Politics* (New York: Public Affairs/Perseus Books, 2004), based on a concept first cited by Nye in a series of works in the 1980s.
6. Daniel Kahnemann and Amos Tversky, *Choices, Values, and Frames* (New York: Russell Sage Foundation, 2000).
7. Nassim Nicholas Taleb, *The Black Swan: The Impact of the Highly Improbable* (New York: Random House, 2007).
8. Joshua Cooper Ramo, *The Age of the Unthinkable: Why the New World Disorder Constantly Surprises Us and What We Can Do About It* (New York: Back Bay, 2010).
9. Thomas S. Kuhn and Ian Hacking, *The Structure of Scientific Revolutions* (Chicago: University of Chicago Press, 2012).

American Jews Speak a "Jewish Language," by Dr. Sarah Bunin Benor

1. My thinking on this has been influenced by several scholars, including David Gold, Sol Steinmetz, Joshua A. Fishman, and Chaim Weiser. For details, see Sarah Bunin Benor, "Do American Jews Speak a 'Jewish Language'? A Model of Jewish Linguistic Distinctiveness," *Jewish Quarterly Review* 99, no. 2 (2009): 230–69.
2. Leon Wieseltier, "Language, Identity, and the Scandal of American Jewry," *Journal of Jewish Communal Service* 86, nos. 1–2 (2011): 14–22.

The Tones of Leadership, by Dr. David Bryfman

1. A. H. Early and B. T. Johnson, "Gender and Leadership Style: A Meta-Analysis," *Psychological Bulletin* 108, no. 2 (1990): 233–56.
2. Francesca Donner, "Everyone's a Critic, But Delivery Still Counts," *Wall Street Journal*, September 24, 2014, http://blogs.wsj.com/atwork /2014/09/24/everyones-a-critic-but-style-counts/.

Orthodox Jewish Feminism on the Rise: Offense Is Your Best Defense, by Dr. Sharon Weiss-Greenberg

1. An *agunah* is a particularly vexing matter for Jewish feminists. Jewish law classifies as *agunah* (lit. "chained") women whose husbands (for example) have disappeared (perhaps in battle) and who have not (and cannot now) give their wives a *get*, a bill of divorce. Such women are chained to their former marriage and cannot remarry.

Model-Driven or Market-Driven? A Lesson from Birthright Israel, by Dr. Shaul Kelner

1. Theodore Sasson, "American Jewish Attachment to Israel Resilient," *Tablet*, October 1, 2013, www.tabletmag.com/scroll/147231 /american-jewish-attachment-to-israel-resilient.
2. Barry Chazan, *Does the Teen Israel Experience Make a Difference?* (New York: Israel Experience Inc., 1997); Shaul Kelner, *Tours That Bind: Diaspora, Pilgrimage and Israeli Birthright Tourism* (New York: New York University Press, 2010), 7, 31–44.
3. Barry Chazan, "The Israel Trip: A New Form of Jewish Education," in *Youth Trips to Israel: Rationale and Realization* (New York: CRB Foundation and the Mandell L. Berman Jewish Heritage Center as JESNA, 1994), A1–A26; Kelner, *Tours That Bind*, 36–38.
4. Charles Kadushin, Shaul Kelner, and Leonard Saxe, *Being a Jewish Teenager in America: Trying to Make It* (Waltham, MA: Brandeis University, Cohen Center for Modern Jewish Studies, 2000), 27–28.

Les Wexner, Harry Truman, and the Leadership of Readership, by David Gergen

1. John W. Gardner, *On Leadership* (New York: Free Press, 1990), 165.
2. Fred Kaplan, *Lincoln: The Biography of a Writer* (New York: HarperCollins, 2008).
3. Michael T. Benson, *Harry S. Truman and the Founding of Israel* (Westport, CT: Praeger, 1997), 53.
4. Ibid., 30.